NEW VISION,
NEW DIRECTIONS

To my Mother, Olivia L. Hater

Shortly after I began the first grade in St. William's School, the doctor told you that I would have to stay home from school for six months to recover from an illness. During that time, you taught me every subject, every day. From you, I received my first formal religious instruction from the *Baltimore Catechism*. Throughout my life, you have continued to teach me the ways of God. From you, I received my initial fervor to evangelize and catechize.

Thanks, Mom, for your love, wisdom, intelligence, patience, and devotion. May I respond to the needs of God's people as you always respond to my needs and those of our family, friends, and neighbors.

In thanksgiving for all you are to me, I dedicate this book on the *Catechism of the Catholic Church* to you. May God give you health, happiness, love, peace, and joy.

NEW VISION, NEW DIRECTIONS

IMPLEMENTING THE
CATECHISM OF THE CATHOLIC CHURCH

FOREWORD BY
ARCHBISHOP DANIEL E. PILARCZYK

ROBERT J. HATER

ThomasMore
A DIVISION OF TABOR PUBLISHING
ALLEN, TEXAS • CHICAGO, ILLINOIS

NIHIL OBSTAT
Reverend Robert L. Hagedorn
Censor Librorum

June 24, 1994

IMPRIMATUR
†Most Reverend Carl K. Moeddel
Vicar General and Auxiliary Bishop of the Archdiocese of Cincinnati

June 27, 1994

The *Nihil Obstat* and *Imprimatur* are official declarations that the work contains nothing contrary to Faith and Morals. It is not implied thereby that those granting the *Nihil Obstat* and *Imprimatur* agree with the contents, statements, or opinions expressed.

ACKNOWLEDGEMENTS
Scripture quotations are taken from *The Jerusalem Bible,* copyright © 1966 by Darton, Longman & Todd, Ltd. and Doubleday & Company, Inc.

Excerpts from the English translation of the *Catechism of the Catholic Church* for the United States of America, copyright © 1994, United States Catholic Conference, Inc.—Liberia Editrice Vaticana.

COVER ART: Pin Yi Wu

Send all inquiries to:
Tabor Publishing
200 East Bethany Drive
Allen, Texas 73002–3804

Printed in the United States of America

ISBN 0–88347–283–X

1 2 3 4 5 6   98 97 96 95 94

CONTENTS

CONTENTS

FOREWORD

When something unexpected occurs, we are inclined to ask "What happened?" This is the first thing on people's lips after an explosion, when they wake up in the hospital, or when they hear troubling or exciting news about a loved one. Lots of people have been asking "What happened?" about religious education in the Church over the last several decades.

It is not that religious education is some kind of a hospital or explosion, but rather that it is an important and beloved aspect of people's faith life. Some of us look back to the "good old days" of the *Baltimore Catechism*, others look back to "the good old days" when the equivalence of memorization and religious education was overcome by new approaches after the Second Vatican Council. Some look back to "the good old days" when religious educators who did not seem to care anything about content were brought to task through the vigilance of the Church and its leaders. In every case, people wondered what happened. Now, the Church has issued the *Catechism of the Catholic Church*. Again, we are inclined to ask what happened to bring this about, what happened to catechetics in the course of the preparation of the *Catechism*, what will happen now that the *Catechism* is in place.

Father Robert Hater in this book talks a lot about what happened in various contexts of religious education since before the council. He also has a lot to say about why these things happened, and about how the happenings of the past are going to influence religious education of the future.

As a diocesan bishop, I welcome the appearance of *Catechism of the Catholic Church*, and I also welcome the appearance of this book by a loyal priest of our archdiocese who has a wide background in religious education. I think Father Hater's book will help religious educators and other Catholics understand the significance of the *Catechism* and use it for the purpose for which it was intended. My hope is that the *Catechism* wins wide and enthusiastic acceptance and that wise religious educators, like Father Hater, help the Church to digest it and be strengthened by it.

Most Reverend Daniel E. Pilarczyk
Archbishop of Cincinnati

P R E F A C E

Why should you even consider reading another piece of literature about the *Catechism of the Catholic Church*?! Within the same Church some of us have looked upon the coming of the *Catechism* with eager anticipation and others with a bit of apprehension. Through the pages of this book the author shares with us a life-giving approach to this catechetical event. This book is about catechetical renewal, conversion, and practical ideas for using the *Catechism*.

In *Catechesi Tradendae*, John Paul II calls for the continuing renewal of catechesis (#17). Through this book Father Hater makes an excellent contribution to this endeavor for our time. A person new to religious education will find a good history of the last twenty-five years in this field. Veterans will resonate with the description and realize that it puts structure on their experience. With this preparation we can begin to look at new directions.

Adult educators are asking the question, "How can we make the doctrine of our Church accessible to our adult members?" These pages share with us a model for understanding how this might occur. One is given insights into conversion. Adult educators will only need to bring their creativity to the development of processes for inviting adults to consider the relevancy of the Church's doctrine for their lives.

Are you a person who is looking for some very practical ideas on how the *Catechism* might be of use to you in your ministry? The pages of this book will not let you down in this regard either.

The author of these pages, Father Robert Hater, is well qualified to reflect on new directions in catechesis. For the last twenty years he has been in the midst of the ministry of religious education. He has been a diocesan director of religious education and a professor of religious studies. He is a storyteller and an educator. The reading of this book is not a dull chore nor an intellectual nightmare! Profound though it is, it comes from the "pen" of a good teacher.

This book was commissioned by the National Conference of Catechetical Leadership (NCCL) as part of its ongoing effort to assist with the implementation of the *Catechism of the Catholic Church*. We are grateful to Tabor Publishing and, especially, Eileen Anderson for making this endeavor possible.

Marilyn Kerber, SND de N

Director of Religious Education,
Archdiocese of Cincinnati
President,
National Conference
of Catechetical Leadership

INTRODUCTION

T hose who with God's help have welcomed
Christ's call and freely responded to it are urged
on by love of Christ to proclaim the Good News
everywhere in the world. This treasure, received from
the apostles, has been faithfully guarded by their
successors. All Christ's faithful are called to hand it on
from generation to generation, by professing the faith,
by living it in fraternal sharing, and by celebrating it in
liturgy and prayer.

Catechism of the Catholic Church[1]

Yesterday, Helen celebrated her ninetieth birthday. I first met
her almost twenty-five years ago, when her daughter asked me
to preside at a home Mass for her birthday. Subsequently, we
celebrated her birthday with a home Mass every five years.

This time, Helen wanted to celebrate her birthday at the
Saturday afternoon liturgy in the parish that nurtured her since

---

[1] *Prologue, #3.*

she joined it in 1935. Many of her family and friends, including her children, grandchildren, and great grandchildren attended.

I presided at the liturgy, which took place on the Sunday before Ascension. In the Gospel, Jesus spoke about returning to heaven and promised not to leave us strangers. He promised to send the Holy Spirit and dwell in the lives of his followers. During my homily, I recalled how his promise was fulfilled in the family members and friends that had gathered for Helen's celebration.

Later, at a dinner in her honor, the family recalled happy times, sang Irish songs, and enjoyed themselves. Her daughter reminisced about Helen's witness to their Catholic faith. Then, looking around the room, Helen said, "My prayer every day is that all of those in whom my blood flows, might, one day, see the face of God in Heaven."

Experiencing this family together enfleshed Jesus' words in the afternoon's Gospel, "I will not leave you orphans." In Helen's family I saw Jesus' story (The Story), repeated in common lore of her family and friends (the stories). In these stories they learned what it means to be human, Christian, and Catholic.

Helen's birthday celebration focused my thoughts as I write this introduction, for it expressed the heart of this book; namely: life's ultimate goal is to "see the face of God."

Jesus taught us what we must do to gain eternal life, and Christian families reveal God's ongoing presence. All Church ministry, including catechesis, reinforces this goal, revealed in the stories of faithful people. For Christians, this demands knowing, accepting, and living Jesus' story in today's complex society.

This book suggests how catechesis can "echo" Jesus' story. Within the context of Jesus' story, catechesis is a process that invites a person to hear, understand, interiorize, and respond to

God's Word in acts of service and celebration.[2] It is specifically concerned with applying the instructional aspect of Jesus' message in a way that leads to conversion.

In catechesis, it is necessary to distinguish between content (what is taught) and method (how the content is taught). Major changes in religious education during the past twenty-five years happened in these areas. These changes were initiated because catechetical methods that worked effectively before Vatican II were no longer adequate.

Following the council, religious educators struggled to clarify basic Catholic teaching (content) and devise new ways to teach it (method). As this happened, they developed their understanding of the need for solid content and effective methodology. They saw that good instruction about the basics of the faith is integral to effective catechetical methodology.

As the post-Vatican II Church reached out to the world, religious educators realized that the challenges to catechesis from secular society cannot be minimized. They also saw that effective methods for adapting Jesus' story to various situations alone will not solve today's catechetical challenges, for the issues involved are primarily culture, family, and Church issues. Unless catechists acknowledge the real situation of people today, neither solid content nor good methodology will produce much fruit.

---

2 *Catechesi Tradendae* (CT), #18, says, "Catechesis is an education of children, young people and adults in the faith which includes especially the teaching of Christian doctrine imparted, generally speaking in an organic and systematic way, with a view to initiating hearers into the fullness of Christian life." *The National Catechetical Directory* (NCD), in #5, describes catechesis as "efforts which help individuals and communities acquire and deepen Christian faith and identity through initiation rites, instruction, and formation of conscience."

To get a clearer picture of the current catechetical climate, this book considers today's situation in light of challenges and opportunities afforded by the *Catechism of the Catholic Church*. **Chapter One** gives a historical review of religious education in the Catholic Church from the middle of the twentieth century until today. It considers the pre-Vatican II Church as a relatively closed society and examines the religious instruction method of the *Baltimore Catechism*. Next, it looks at the dynamics released at Vatican II as the Church shifted to a more open society. A consideration of what happened in catechesis from the time of the council until today highlights this section. **Chapter Two** considers the *Catechism of the Catholic Church* in reference to the content of Jesus' story, the Catholic story, conversion, and effective methodology. **Chapter Three** looks at today's catechetical challenge in light of contemporary United States cultural dynamics, aspects of contemporary culture, and contemporary needs. **Chapter Four** suggests future directions in view of where the Church has been and where it hopes to go in the twenty-first century.

I give special acknowledgments and thanks to my mother, Olivia Hater, for her support and encouragement while I wrote this book, and to Archbishop Daniel E. Pilarczyk for his helpful foreword. I feel honored that he took the time personally to read my book and offer many useful suggestions as I finalized it. I also am grateful to Sister Marilyn Kerber for her fine preface and insightful analysis of the draft manuscript. I also thank Neil Parent, executive director of the National Conference of Catechetical Leadership Office (NCCL) and Richard Reichert, chair of the NCCL Publications Committee, for their help in every phase of the book's formulation and publication. I thank, also, the readers of the draft version, identified through the NCCL network, namely, James DeBoy, Carole Eipers, Barbara Anne Radtke, and Thomas Walters, for their useful critiques and suggestions.

I am grateful to the National Conference of Catechetical Leadership for sponsoring this book and allowing me to modify and use again parts of previously published works that I wrote for them, namely, *Religious Education and Catechesis: A Shift in Focus* and *The Relationship between Evangelization and Catechesis* in pages 17–25 of this work. I also thank the Office of Publications of the United States Catholic Conference for allowing me to use again, in pages 55–73 of this book, certain sections of my previously published article "Facilitating Conversion Processes" (*Christian Adulthood*, 1967, pp. 3–15).

This book hopes to reflect Pope John Paul II's wisdom, in his introduction to the *Catechism of the Catholic Church*, that

> In reading the *Catechism of the Catholic Church* we can perceive the wonderful unity of the mystery of God, his saving will, as well as the central place of Jesus Christ, the only-begotten Son of God, sent by the Father, made man in the womb of the Blessed Virgin Mary by the power of the Holy Spirit, to be our Savior. Having died and risen, Christ is always present in his Church, especially in the sacraments; he is the source of our faith, the model of Christian behavior and the Master of our prayer.[3]

---

[3] Pope John Paul II, Introduction, *Catechism of the Catholic Church*, #2.

CHAPTER ONE

RELIGIOUS INSTRUCTION IN THE CATHOLIC CHURCH: 1950S UNTIL TODAY

My earliest recollection of religion class pictures me standing with other students along a wall in a second grade classroom answering *Baltimore Catechism* questions.

I recall the day that Sister Mary quizzed us, "Who is God?" "Why did God make you?" I felt good when I gave the correct answer to the first question but bad when she told me my second answer was not exact and instructed me to sit down. Those who gave all correct answers received a holy card.

By the fourth grade I knew all the answers in *Baltimore Catechism* #1 for children; by the eighth grade, all the answers in *Baltimore Catechism* #2 for youth; and by the senior year in high school, all the answers in *Baltimore Catechism* #3 for adults. At this time, I figured I knew all the religion I needed to answer my questions and defend my faith.

My experiences were not unique. Many Catholics, instructed before Vatican II, learned their faith the same way. After my ordination, I used the *Baltimore Catechism* to teach the Catholic faith in Confraternity of Christian Doctrine (CCD) classes and in Catholic high schools.

This chapter addresses two points. First, it explains the overall dynamics operative in closed and open societies, as the background to help clarify what happened in the Church after Vatican II. Second, it looks at the consequences of the changes brought about by Vatican II.

I. VATICAN II: TRANSFORMATION FROM A CLOSED TO AN OPEN SOCIETY

Sociologists classify a society as closed or open depending on the degree to which energy, opinions, and ideas flow freely in and outside of them.

A *closed* society maintains much of its energy and dynamics within the group itself. There is only a limited flow of energy between a closed society and the outside world, and what energy or actions are exchanged with the larger group is well controlled by the dynamics within the closed society.' Considered schematically, the dynamics operative in a closed society can be pictured in the following way:

The pre-Vatican II Church was a relatively closed society. There was significant contact, however, with the world, illustrated by the broken lines in the above diagram. Even though Catholics lived and worked with people of various religious denominations, the narrowly confined dynamics of the Church influenced *how* they related to the broader society. These dynamics influenced the Catholic attitude toward the world and personal and Church relationships with other religious denominations. This is illustrated by experiences from my and my mother's childhoods. Mom told me that as a child she was not permitted to play with the girl across the street because this girl was a Protestant. In my boyhood, the injunction was

not so severe; I played with the Protestants in our neighborhood, but was forbidden to go into their Church.

In an *open* society, a free flow of energy happens within
and without the group. Hence, the energies of various societies
or groups significantly influence each other. This can be
pictured in the following way:

OUTSIDE WORLD   CHURCH   OUTSIDE WORLD

The United States, in contrast to totalitarian countries, is
an open society. Here people enjoy freedom and are not con-
strained to follow one particular ideology.

Every family, organization, group, or church falls some-
where on a spectrum between a closed and open society.

Pre-Vatican II Catholic Church: A Relatively Closed Society

The pre-Vatican II Catholic Church was a relatively closed society. A pipeline of salvation went from God through the church's
hierarchy to its members. Hence, the pope, bishops, and priests
gave instructions through doctrines and directives and the laity
were expected to obey. Sometimes, church rules were seen as
directives which had to be followed for the people to be saved.
In this system, fear and guilt were strong motivating factors.

Since church teachings contained the blueprint for salvation, they were to be learned and accepted totally. Little room
for doubt was possible, for doubting church teaching was
tantamount to doubting God.

The *Baltimore Catechism*'s influence happened within the context of the church as a closed system. It was the chief way to teach the basics of Catholic faith to the uninitiated, especially to children and youth. This relatively closed Catholic world often portrayed God as a strict judge and Jesus as the divine Son of God. These images took precedence over images of God as a loving creator and Jesus as a friend. Latin language in church services preserved an other-worldly mystique and frequent confession kept Catholics faithful to church teachings. The *Baltimore Catechism* held sway over the minds and hearts of Catholics as long as the church remained a relatively closed system.

Post-Vatican II Catholic Church: A Relatively Open Society

Even though the pre-Vatican II church was a relatively closed society, nonetheless it was a part of the broader society. Consequently, worldwide societal changes affected the church, set the stage for Vatican II, and influenced church leaders to shift the church's focus from a relatively closed to an relatively open society. As Vatican II updated the church, no one expected the explosion that happened when the council changed the Latin Mass, questioned age-old Catholic ways of doing things, and refocused the church's responsibility in the world.

The *Constitution on the Sacred Liturgy* changed the closed ritualistic system of Catholicism by encouraging inculturation within Catholic worship. The *Dogmatic Constitution on the Church* moved away from the church as hierarchy to the church as a Christian community. It admitted that the church of Christ is found in other Christian denominations and also acknowledged God's presence in the great world religions. The *Dogmatic Constitution on Divine Revelation* stressed the importance of the Scriptures. The *Declaration on Religious Freedom* underscored the right to religious freedom, while the *Pastoral Constitution on the Church in the Modern World* challenged Christians to transform society by the power of the gospel.

4

These documents brought about many changes. In the emerging church that followed Vatican II, much of the old system no longer worked. Catechism lists of what must be done or not done no longer sufficed, as Catholics discovered the wisdom of the Scriptures and judged church directives by new standards. In this process, the former institutional identity of the church changed, as Catholics focused on the church as a community of faith.

Catholic leaders often were unprepared to cope with the changing dynamics caused when the church entered into dialogue with the world. Now, in an open society, the church's influence entered the broader society:

WORLD   CHURCH   WORLD

And the broader society's influence also entered the church:

WORLD   CHURCH   WORLD

Movements in this latter direction exposed Catholic parishes and diocesan organizations to challenges which they did not experience previously. This openness changed religious communities as men and women, formerly confined to convents, seminaries, and monasteries, entered into dialogue with the broader society. Catholics took leadership roles in the struggles for social justice and equal rights. In ecumenical affairs, challenging questions surfaced in dealing with Jews, Protestants, and members of other religions. Such new directions required the refocusing of church personnel and structures to serve the complex situation that was emerging.

II. CONSEQUENCES FOR RELIGIOUS EDUCATION

The dynamics that were unleashed influenced every aspect of church life. The changes that emerged pointed to the limitations of pre-Vatican II catechesis in a post–Vatican II church and affected the future orientation of religious education. Five consequences for religious education followed from these changes.

Shifting Focus of Religious Education

Moving to an open society inclined Catholics to look anew at the content and methods of religious education. The council spoke of church teachings (content) in terms of God's love, Jesus' humanity/divinity, and church community. While consistent with past Catholic traditions, these notions represented departures from the way the church presented these doctrines immediately before Vatican II.

Now Catholics learned that Jesus proclaimed the reign (kingdom) of God which exists wherever God is present. This includes God's presence in society, other Christian denominations, and the great world religions. In this perspective, the church as a whole, not ordained ministry, becomes the chief focus of God's presence and of the grace needed for salvation. Ordained ministers are servant leaders, called to insure the church's faithfulness to traditions coming from Jesus. The church's missionary goal is to proclaim God's reign.

The consequences for Catholics were far-ranging. In particular, lay people were encouraged to become "adults" in their faith, take responsibility for their religious lives, and transform society in light of the gospel.

While this happened, attitudes toward church authority changed, as Catholics relied more on their own consciences to make personal moral decisions. This was illustrated in particular by Catholic reaction to Pope Paul VI's *Humanae Vitae (On Human Life)*, which reiterated the church's traditional ban on artificial birth control. The disregard by many Catholics of Pope Paul's teaching in this document represented a significant shift in the way they responded to church teaching when it differed from their personal viewpoints.

Many Catholics, caught in the turmoil after Vatican II, asked, "Which truths are unchangeable and which can change?" Two aspects of Catholic life popularly thought to be unchangeable—the Latin Mass and Friday abstinence—changed. If these could change, Catholics often wondered, what was unchangeable? In other words, they began to ask, "What does it mean to be Catholic?" This question illustrated the identity crisis among many Catholics with regard to essential Catholic belief and practice.

Such uncertainty affected the teaching of religion in Catholic schools and parishes. Catechists and parents struggled to find effective ways to teach religion, especially to children and youth. Some teachers abandoned the *Baltimore Catechism* as they searched for more creative ways to share the faith. Other teachers held on to it. Such differences of approach caused considerable consternation among pastors, teachers, and parents.

The negative image of the *Baltimore Catechism* among some Catholic educators has lasted. This explains, in part, their resistance to the *Catechism of the Catholic Church*.

During this time, adult education began to be stressed, as catechists came to appreciate the relationship between developmental stages of psychology and growth in faith. Religious educators also saw how viewing creation as an ongoing process sheds new light on human responsibility to build the earth and how culture and historical circumstances influence communal and individual faith.

As this happened, human experience and new methods often took precedence over teaching content or basic beliefs. This can be explained, in part, as a reaction to the emphasis on content during the *Baltimore Catechism* era. At the same time, however, many catechists began to integrate content within an effective catechetical process.

New Ministries—Director of Religious Education and Diocesan Religious Education Offices

In the late 1960s and early 1970s, a new ministry, the director of religious education (DRE), developed in the Catholic community to address the changing climate in religious education. Those who took up this ministry, largely sisters at first, coordinated parish religious education and performed many other functions. Many served full-time in this new ministry; many others, however, did so in a part-time or volunteer capacity.

Some dioceses formed religious education offices, independent of Catholic school offices. Before this time, diocesan CCD programs generally operated under Catholic school offices.

Often, religious educators on diocesan and parish levels were involved in a wide variety of pastoral activities. These included: liturgical preparation, counseling, youth retreats, vocation work, social justice movements, and ministry to divorced and alienated Catholics. In fact, many of the above ministries had their roots in work done by religious educators in the 1970s.

In the 1980s, some religious educators began to specify their ministry by using the language of catechesis. The terms "catechist" or "catechetical leader" began to replace "religion teacher," "religious educator," or "director of religious education"

in many parishes and dioceses. As the role of the religious educator became clarified, increasing importance was given to the
catechetical context of this ministry.

Several factors influenced the movement to the language
of catechesis. These factors included: (1) the inability of religious educators to do everything required of them within the
wider scope of the ministry that many of them had assumed,
(2) the need to clarify the proper role of religious education
within the context of the new ministries emerging in the
Catholic community, and (3) the use of the language of catechesis, not religious education, in official church documents.[4]

As new ministries emerged, many "turf" struggles took
place. Often, these ministries overlapped with catechesis. Then,
new questions surfaced, like: (1) Who is responsible for the religious formation of youth, the catechist or the youth minister?
(2) How do catechists and liturgists specify their responsibilities, when working in the same ministerial area, like First
Commu-nion preparation? (3) How do diocesan family life and
religious education offices relate on matters that pertain to family catechesis? Gradually, such questions clarified as ministry, in
general, and catechetical ministry, in particular, came into
sharper focus.

During the 1980s, as some of the work, previously done
by religious educators, was taken up by other ministers, catechists found new directions for their ministry in *Evangelii
Nuntiandi, Catechesi Tradendae*, the *Rite of Christian Initiation
of Adults (RCIA)*, and many other church and professional
publications.

---

[4] Five documents, in particular, published in the 1970s clarified this direction.
They were: (1) *General Catechetical Directory* (1971); (2) *Rite of Christian
Initiation of Adults* (1972); (3) Pope Paul VI, *Evangelii Nuntiandi* (*Apostolic
Exhortation on Evangelization*), 1975; (4) the National Catechetical Directory
entitled *Sharing the Light of Faith* (1978); and (5) Pope John Paul II, *Catechesi
Tradendae* (*Apostolic Exhortation on Catechesis*), 1979. These documents came at
a time when many religious educators were overwhelmed by the responsibilities
and pressures placed on them. Their own experiences and these documents
affected the changing climate of religious education in the 1980s.

New Directions in Catechesis

During the 1970s, as the church adapted to the post-Vatican II theology, teaching the basics of the faith often became blurred. As this happened, many grey areas surfaced, since some interpretations of the emerging Catholic story were not consistent or precise. Hence, the message of Catholicism often was unclear or lost in the midst of sharing sessions, collages, and experiential events.

In the early 1980s, a clearer picture emerged and catechists, parents, priests, and the hierarchy saw the need to strengthen the content of religious instruction. This occurred at the same time that solid methods for teaching religion, often included under the general expression "the catechetical process," were being developed. These methods linked teaching the content of Catholic belief and practice to a person's everyday life. Such new developments were incorporated into the catechetical life of the Catholic community.

As this happened, catechists learned more about how God's Word is communicated. The following perspectives emerged from efforts to further this communication.

- Emphasize Scripture and basic Catholic teaching in all catechesis.
- Begin catechesis at birth and continue it until death.
- Emphasize the importance of adult catechesis.
- Acknowledge people's cultures, life situations, and experiences.
- Strive to meet people's spiritual needs.
- Center catechetical activities on initiating people into a faith community.
- Incorporate the justice dimension of the gospel into all catechetical activities.
- Specify the role of catechesis and link it with the new pastoral ministries emerging in the church.

- Use the catechetical process in systematic catechesis.[5]
- Acknowledge the ecumenical scope of catechetical ministry.
- Implement Catholic education through various models, one of which is a Catholic school model.
- Clarify religious education/catechetical language, opting for the language of catechesis.

These perspectives moved catechetical leaders to see the following:

- The entire community—family, parish, school, diocesan staff—forms the basis for catechetical ministry.
- All communities, including families, religious communities, parishes, and diocese, are responsible to prepare people for leadership roles in catechetical ministry.
- Catechists work with other pastoral ministers to carry out the mission of Christ and the church.
- Catechists are experts in their ministry, which is limited in scope.
- Good catechesis is responsive to local community needs, while recognizing how a local community relates to the larger church.
- Parents play a vital role in the catechesis of family members.
- Parishes, schools, and dioceses need to place high priority on working with parents and on other forms of adult education.

While these clarifications were happening, many Catholics recognized more clearly how God is present in all

---

[5] For an explanation of the catechetical process, see footnote 16.

creation and prepared themselves to take a responsible role in secular society. This preparation often happened through small group sharing sessions, like Christ Renews His Parish, RENEW, Marriage Encounter, the Charismatic movement, and Scripture study groups, as well as through other parish renewal efforts, diocesan ministry, and catechetical programs.

As Catholic renewal proceeded, church members felt the trauma of change, the demands of freedom, and the responsibilities of conscience, while learning more effective ways to relate with the secular world and other religious denominations. The church stood at a turning point and took another look at how the Christian community influences the lifelong process of coming to faith. As this happened, Catholics discovered anew the implications of evangelization for catechetical ministry.

Evangelization and Catechesis

The work of clarifying the proper role of catechetical ministry was assisted by new developments in Catholic evangelization. The incentive for these developments came from Pope Paul VI's *Evangelii Nuntiandi*, published in 1973.[6] This pioneering work was not taken up seriously by the Catholic community until the 1980s. In it, catechists saw the important role that evangelization plays in the church's catechetical ministry.

Following the leadership of Pope Paul VI in *Evangelii Nuntiandi* and Pope John Paul II in *Catechesi Tradendae*, catechesis began to be viewed as an element or moment in the evangelization/conversion process.[7] This process is rooted in the Christian community, where the Lord continues to proclaim the message of God's love. Seen in this context, evangelization is an ongoing process within the Christian community that seeks to initiate people ever more deeply into the mystery of God's love (i.e., the reign or kingdom of God) as it is manifested most fully in the dying and rising of Jesus.

[6] Pope Paul VI, *Evangelization in the Modern World*, USCC, 1973.
[7] John Paul II, *On Catechesis in Our Time*, USCC, 1979.

Hence, evangelization came to be seen as the energizing center of all pastoral ministries, including catechesis. Pope Paul VI emphasizes this point by calling evangelization the "essential mission of the Church."[8] It provides the motivating force for all church ministries and is intimately related to them.

Catechesis has a special relationship to evangelization, which is the foundation and source of all catechesis. *Catechesi Tradendae* relates catechesis to evangelization in the following way:

> Evangelization—which has the aim of bringing the good news to the whole of humanity, so that all may live by it—is a rich, complex, and dynamic reality, made up of elements, or one could say moments, that are essential and different form each other, and that must all be kept in view simultaneously. Catechesis is one of these moments—a very remarkable one—in the whole process of evangelization.[9]

Although they can be described separately, catechesis cannot exist without evangelization, for its content is the same as the content of evangelization, namely, the person and gospel of Jesus Christ.[10] Consequently,

> Within the whole process of evangelization, the aim of cate-chesis is to be the teaching and maturation stage, that is to say, the period in which the Christian, having accepted by faith the person of Jesus Christ as the one Lord and having given him complete adherence by sincere conversion of heart, endeavors to know better this Jesus to whom he has entrusted himself: to know his "mystery," the kingdom of God pro-claimed by him, the requirements and promises contained in his Gospel message and the paths that he has laid down for anyone who wishes to follow him.[11]

Catechesis, rooted in evangelization, is an important way that the Christian community assists people on their spiritual

[8] Pope John Paul II, *On Evangelization in the Modern World*, #14.
[9] CT, #18.
[10] Cf. CT, #18.
[11] CT, #31.

journey. Along this journey, catechesis is only one aspect, but a vital one, in the church's overall evangelizing ministry, for catechesis emphasizes *understanding* the mystery of Christ, which necessitates *teaching* the message of Jesus and the church in a clear, correct way.[12] In this context, Pope John Paul II says,

> Catechesis is an education of children, young people and adults in the faith which includes especially the teaching of Christian doctrine imparted, generally speaking in an organic and systematic way, with a view to initiating the hearers into the fullness of Christian life.[13]

Clarifying this relationship between evangelization and catechesis puts catechetical activities and relationships with other pastoral ministries on a firm basis. The special relationship that catechesis has with evangelization can be summarized as follows:

- The evangelization/conversion process, based in community, is the foundation and source of all catechesis.
- Informal catechesis, a natural concomitant to evangelization, is the ongoing responsibility of all Christians.[14]
- Systematic catechesis, an important aspect of evangelization, springs from and flows back to informal catechesis.[15]
- The catechetical process is the general methodology that systematic catechesis employs.[16]

---

[12] Cf. CT, #20.

[13] CT, #18.

[14] Informal catechesis includes those pastoral activities—family prayer, speaking of God's love, community building, evangelizing activities, service projects, liturgy—which, even if not intended primarily to catechize, have a catechetical aspect. To qualify as catechesis, these activities have to relate in some way to God and the Christian story.

Focusing on the relationship between evangelization and catechesis made it easier for catechists to see that conversion is lifelong and that Jesus' message must be related to a person's life situation and experiences. This perception led them to stress Scriptures and to incorporate the gospel's justice dimension into all catechetical activities. At the same time, it helped catechists see the importance of taking into account the psychological and spiritual state of those being catechized.

Gradually, as catechists learned better ways to balance content and method, it became obvious that conversion and methods to help facilitate it are not the same. The goal of catechesis is conversion, but there are many methods to help facilitate it. Within the context of conversion, it also became clear that knowledge about one's faith (content or message) is a very important part of conversion.

Catechesis and the Rite of Christian Initiation of Adults

The *Rite of Christian Initiation of Adults (RCIA)*, published in provisional form in 1972 and in final form in 1988, profoundly influenced catechesis. It emphasized in a liturgical context what religious educators saw in a catechetical context, namely, that coming to faith or conversion is a gradual process and that pastoral ministry must be sensitive to the various faith levels of those being catechized. It also stressed that conversion happens in the midst of a community—family, parish, religious order, or small faith community.

---

[15] Systematic catechesis involves any catechetical activities that aim at calling forth a response to the living Word of God in a deliberate, intentional, and structural way.

[16] The catechetical process is the method that catechesis employs. In today's catechetical climate it takes in to account the situation of the person being catechized and addresses the message to be taught to the person's or persons' human experience. The process encourages the one being catechized to reflect on this message and discover new insights from it which can be integrated into one's life. Such integration leads to a positive response in life and worship.

The *RCIA* influenced adult catechesis as pastoral leaders used various catechetical methods, including lectionary-based catechesis, to instruct catechumens. Some proponents of lectionary-based catechesis argued for using only the texts of the Sunday liturgy as the basis for catechesis in the *RCIA*. Others disagreed, saying this approach fails to give the catechumens an adequate framework to learn the essentials or basics of the Catholic faith. This debate still is not resolved, but it is becoming increasingly clear that more than lectionary-based catechesis alone is needed. In the 1990s, added emphasis was given to adapting the *RCIA* to the Christian initiation of children. In many parishes, this became an effective way to catechize children who were preparing to join the Catholic community.

This chapter has summarized the changing context of catechesis in the aftermath of Vatican II by showing that the emphasis placed on experience and methodology was a natural corrective to the strong emphasis on content before Vatican II.

The 1990s provide an opportunity to continue the positive developments in catechesis since Vatican II. In particular, this involves the relationship between content and method.

The *Catechism of the Catholic Church* will help catechists clarify basic faith beliefs and refine the sound catechetical methods developed in recent years. The *Catechism* challenges catechists to incorporate the best of what has been learned about the catechetical process since Vatican II with the basic teachings of the Catholic Church. They can respond to this challenge by proclaiming the "Good News" of Jesus Christ through solid catechesis and good Christian lives.

Hopefully, in the effort to integrate content and method, catechists will recall the pastoral principle of the *Roman Catechism*, which concludes the Prologue of the *Catechism of the Catholic Church*:

The whole concern of doctrine and its teaching must be directed to the love that never ends. Whether something is proposed for belief, for hope or for action, the love of our Lord must always be made accessible, so that anyone can see that all the works of perfect Christian virtue spring from love and have no other objective than to arrive at love.[17]

---

[17] Prologue, *Catechism of the Catholic Church*, #25, quoting the *Roman Catechism*, Preface, #10.

CATECHISM OF THE CATHOLIC CHURCH, CONVERSION, AND THE CATHOLIC STORY

Many Catholics are curious about the *Catechism of the Catholic Church*. A middle-aged man, remembering the list of sins he memorized in his youth, said he wanted to find out, "What new sins it contains." While he spoke, his son remarked, "The catech . . . what?" The eight-year-old boy didn't have the foggiest idea what a catechism is.

The "Prologue" of the *Catechism* explains its origin:

The Extraordinary Synod of Bishops in 1985 asked "that a catechism or compendium of all Catholic doctrine regarding both faith and morals be composed." The Holy Father, Pope John Paul II, made the Synod's wish his own, acknowledging that "this desire wholly corresponds to a real need of the universal Church and of the particular Churches." He set to motion everything needed to carry out the Synod of the Fathers' wish.[18]

---

[18] *Catechism of the Catholic Church*, #10, quoting the "Final Report," IIBa, 4 of The Extraordinary Synod of Bishops, 1985, and John Paul II, Discourse at the Closing of the Extraordinary Synod of Bishops, December 7, 1985; AAS 781.

For older Catholics, who think of a catechism in terms of the *Baltimore Catechism*, the *Catechism of the Catholic Church* may be a surprise. It is intended as a reference work and looks more like one, rather than looking like a shorter catechism.

To clarify the role of the *Catechism*, an *Informative Dossier*, prepared in the fall of 1992 by the Editorial Commission of the *Catechism of the Catholic Church*, said,

> The *Catechism* is to be seen as a . . . *catechismus major*, that is a catechism meant for the promoters and teachers of catechesis (Pastores), who have the duty to catechize (as compared to the *catechismus minor* meant for those who profit from catechesis: young adults or children). . .[19]

In a similar vein, the *Catechism* states,

> This work is intended primarily for those responsible for catechesis: first of all the bishops, as teachers of the faith and pastors of the Church. It is offered to them as an instrument in fulfilling their responsibility of teaching the People of God. Through the bishops, it is addressed to redactors of catechisms, to priests, and to catechists. It will also be useful reading for all other Christian faithful.[20]

Hence, the *Catechism* is a reference work, intended primarily for bishops, priests, catechetical leaders, catechists, book publishers, and anyone else interested in ascertaining the essential beliefs of the Catholic faith. It is not intended to be used by children in a catechetical class.

To clarify further its role, it helps to remember that after the Council of Trent (1545–1563), the Catholic Church produced a major catechism, the *Catechism of the Council of Trent*. This catechism formed the basis for the eventual publication of small or minor catechisms, such as the *Baltimore Catechism*,

---

[19] *Dossier*, p. 21.

[20] *Catechism of the Catholic Church*, #12.

written in question-answer form and common to generations of Catholics. The *Catechism of the Catholic Church* is intended to serve in a similar capacity in the production of smaller catechisms and catechetical materials.[21]

The *Dossier* says the *Catechism* is intended to teach "the essential and fundamental content of Catholic faith and morals in a complete and summary way."[22] In describing its structure, Pope John Paul II says,

> The plan of this catechism is inspired by the great tradition of catechisms which build catechesis on four pillars: the baptismal profession of faith (the *Creed*), the sacraments of faith, the life of faith (the *Commandments*), and the prayer of the believer (the *Lord's Prayer*).[23]

Consequently, the *Catechism* is divided into four books:

BOOK ONE, "The Profession of Faith," addresses essential aspects of Catholic teaching beginning with God's revelation and humankind's response. Next it expounds on basic elements of the Nicene Creed.

BOOK TWO presents the seven sacraments and other liturgical celebrations under the title of "The Celebration of the Christian Mystery."

BOOK THREE, entitled "Life in Christ," discusses the dignity of the human person, morality, freedom, society, justice, law, grace, and the Ten Commandments.

BOOK FOUR, "Christian Prayer," considers prayer in Christian life, Hebrew and Christian Scriptures, the tradition of prayer, the life of prayer, and the Our Father.[24]

---

[21] The *Dossier* says the *Catechism of the Catholic Church* is to "serve as a point of reference for the preparation of national or diocesan catechisms" (p. 27).

[22] Ibid., p. 21.

[23] *Catechism of the Catholic Church*, #13.

[24] *Dossier*, p. 21.

The *Dossier* infers that not all teachings in the *Catechism* must be held with the same degree of assent by Catholics, although all of them manifest an "organic unity."[25] At the same time, however, neither the *Catechism* nor the *Dossier* says which teachings are of greater or lesser import. In stressing its organic unity, the *Catechism* says, "This catechism is conceived as *an organic presentation* of the Catholic faith in its entirety. It should be seen therefore as a unified whole."[26]

In admitting varying degrees of assent, the *Dossier* does not imply that Catholics are free to pick and choose as they see fit from noninfallible teachings. The *Dogmatic Constitution on the Church* of Vatican II called upon the faithful to offer adherence to church teaching with a ready and respectful allegiance of mind and will in matters of faith and morals, even those matters that are not defined infallibly. This is not the allegiance that is required for infallible teachings, but it is, nonetheless, a fidelity of mind and will that is called for by official church teaching.[27]

In speaking of adult catechesis, *Adult Catechesis in the Christian Community*, developed by the International Council for Catechesis, says, after encouraging catechists to show particular concern for people "living in irregular situations,"

> Above all, one must begin by accepting adults where they are. . . it is essential to keep in mind the specific adults with whom one is working, their cultural background, human and religious needs, their expectations, faith experiences, and their potential. It is also important to be attentive to their marital and professional status.[28]

---

[25] Ibid., p. 24.

[26] *Catechism of the Catholic Church*, #18.

[27] Cf. "Dogmatic Constitution on the Church" (*Lumen Gentium*), #25.

[28] Adult Catechesis in the Christian Community: Some Principles and Guidelines (Vatican City: International Council for Catechesis, 1990), #55-57, reprinted by the USCC, 1992.

Then, the document continues,

> Of fundamental importance is the *dialogical approach* which,
> while recognizing that all are called to the obedience of faith
> (Rm 1, 5), respects the basic freedom and autonomy of adults
> and encourages them to engage in an open and cordial dia-
> logue. In this way they can make known their needs and can
> participate, as they should, as subjects or agents in their own
> catechesis and in that of others.[29]

The *Catechism of the Catholic Church* makes no decisions
about effective methodologies, but leaves this up to the skills,
background, wisdom, and experience of the catechist. In devis-
ing effective methodologies, the *Dossier* encourages catechists to
take seriously the cultural situations of those being catechized,
makes it clear that the *Catechism* avoids methodological applications, and acknowledges other ways to catechize besides using
the *Catechism*. This means parents, catechists, and others are to
devise effective ways to teach basic Catholic beliefs according to
the ages, circumstances, and cultures of those being catechized.[30]
In other words, the *Catechism* affirms the positive developments
in catechetical process that emerged after Vatican II.

In reiterating the importance of adapting the doctrine
contained in the *Catechism of the Catholic Church*, the
Catechism says,

> By design, this *Catechism* does not set out to provide the adap-
> tation of doctrinal presentations and catechetical methods
> required by the differences of culture, age, spiritual maturity,
> and social and ecclesial condition among all those to whom it
> is addressed. Such indispensable adaptations are the responsi-
> bility of particular catechisms and, even more, of those who
> instruct the faithful.[31]

---

[29] Ibid., #57.

[30] *Dossier*, p. 22.

[31] *Catechism of the Catholic Church*, #24.

Finally, the *Dossier* infers that there are limits to the *Catechism*'s use. It says the *Catechism of the Catholic Church* is "one of the means of catechesis, which, in its turn, is one of the ways of carrying out the prophetic ministry, which in union with the priestly and kingly ministries, constitutes the mission of the Church."[32] Although the *Catechism* is a privileged means of catechesis, it is not the only means.

To be appreciated, the *Catechism of the Catholic Church* needs to be interpreted within the Catholic Christian story and within the cultural aspects described in Chapter Three of this book.[33] Consequently, Chapter Two is divided into two sections, "*Catechism of the Catholic Church*, Content and the Catholic Story" and "*Catechism of the Catholic Church*, Conversion and Methods."

I. CONTENT AND THE CATHOLIC STORY

The *Dossier* speaks of the *Catechism of the Catholic Church* as presenting the "essential and fundamental content of the Catholic faith."[34] The "content" of faith includes notions like "God is the creator of the universe," "Jesus is God and human," "There are seven sacraments," and "Jesus is really present in the Eucharist." Such abstract expressions are part of faith, but faith goes much deeper than abstract expressions alone.

The Catholic faith begins in the Christian story. Hence, one cannot read and understand the *Catechism* apart from this story. Neither can a catechist nor anyone else effectively teach it if the teacher does not know the story upon which it is based. Consequently, catechesis begins with the story, as it is revealed in the Hebrew and Christian Scriptures and handed down in the authentic living witness of the Catholic Christian tradition.

---

[32] *Dossier*, p. 28.
[33] See above, p. 80.
[34] *Dossier*, p. 21.

The Christian Story

The Christian story lays the foundation for abstract faith expressions, such as the Nicene or Apostles' Creed. Two principles underlie any analysis of the relationship between the content of Catholic faith belief and the Catholic Christian story.

First Principle: Content Begins with the Story[35]

For Christians this means that the content or basics of faith begin with the Hebrew/Christian story or with God's presence in history. Viewing "content" only in the abstract fails to recognize that revelation always happens within a human situation or story. Hence, teaching content abstractly without linking it to Jesus' story cannot ground faith in the living story that allowed the Christian community to formulate initially the basic message of Jesus and that allows the Christian community to continually reformulate it in succeeding generations.

The *Dossier* clarifies the "content" of the Catholic Christian story by saying, "In the New Testament, the Gospels are the first great 'Catechism' which was transmitted orally and then put into writing."[36] In other words, the early Christian community derived the content of what they believed and how they acted from Jesus. This included his way of acting, preaching, and celebrating. The disciples capsulized his essential message in the Beatitudes, which contain the spirit of the Christian life. The Beatitudes are the life blood of Christianity, and all Catholic teaching must be discerned in light of them.

Catholics, therefore, begin to consider the content of the *Catechism* with the story of Jesus and his words,

---

[35] "Content" means the basic beliefs of a faith, expressed in faith statements, creeds, liturgical worship, or church pronouncements. Normally, "content" refers to what is taught rather than how it is taught.

[36] *Dossier*, p. 11.

> How happy are the poor in spirit;
>> theirs is the kingdom of heaven. . . .
> Happy the gentle;
>> they shall have the earth for their heritage. . . .
> Happy are the merciful;
>> they shall have mercy shown to them. . . .
> Happy are you when people abuse you and persecute
>> you and speak all kinds of calumny against you on
>> my account.
> Rejoice and be glad, for your reward will be great in heaven;
>> that is how they persecuted the prophets before
>> you.[37]

Essential Catholic beliefs came from Jesus' teachings. These beliefs were centered around his teachings on the reign of God. Early apostles and community leaders felt a responsibility to preserve complete and intact Jesus' teachings. This conviction led the author of Matthew's Gospel to write Jesus' command at the conclusion of this Gospel:

> Teach them to observe all the commandments I give you. And know that I am with you always; yes, to the end of time.[38]

To fulfill their responsibility to carry on Jesus' teachings, the early church opposed heresy and unsound teachings. In succeeding centuries church leaders continued this tradition.

From earliest times, Jesus' story became the church's story. The *Catechism* says,

> The transmission of the Christian faith consists primarily in proclaiming Jesus Christ in order to lead others to faith in him. From the beginning, the first disciples burned with the desire to proclaim Christ: "We cannot but speak of what we

---

[37] Matthew 5:1–12.

[38] Matthew 28:20.

have seen and heard." And they invite people of every era to enter into the joy of their communion with Christ.[39]

Christians of every generation are obliged to center their teachings on the person of Jesus. The *Catechism* says,

> To catechize is "to reveal in the Person of Christ the whole of God's eternal design reaching fulfillment in that Person. It is to seek to understand the meaning of Christ's actions and words and of the signs worked by him." [40]

This statement points out the importance of seeing the content of the *Catechism* within the context of Jesus' teaching on the reign of God, his personal story, and the Christian tradition. It also leads to the second principle in analyzing the relationship between content and story.

Second Principle: The Story Begins with Experience

Christian Scriptures came from the faith experiences of Jesus' followers as they interpreted his words and actions. Faith was their response to him; their saying "amen" to his way. The "what" (content) of their message came from who he was and how they responded to him. Hence, Christian Scriptures are interpreted faith reflections, not abstract principles direct from the mouth of God.[41]

---

[39] *Catechism of the Catholic Church*, #420.

[40] Ibid., #426, quoting CT5.

[41] This section presupposes stages of scriptural development influenced by the faith of the early Christian community as this faith was interpreted by the knowledge and wisdom of the community itself and as it was influenced by the cultural milieu. In other words, the "Jesus Story" contains developmental aspects based on the experience of the earthly Jesus and the experiences of the communities that framed the story.

Understanding this is critical in analyzing the essential content of the Catholic faith. As such, content has to be interpreted within the framework of the Catholic Christian story. Such interpretation gives the clearest indication of what is within the scope of Catholic belief and what is not.

This does not imply that Catholic belief and practice always have been well-balanced. History recounts many instances of imbalanced emphases; for example, stressing the divinity of Christ while neglecting his humanity, or failing to see God's workings in other Christian or world religions.

It does not imply, either, that because something has not been taught or practiced in the past it must be excluded automatically in the future. To insure faithfulness to Jesus' message requires knowledge of Catholic tradition, serious consideration of magisterial teaching, painstaking research, prayer, and openness to the Spirit, remembering that the Spirit is present in the entire Catholic community. In this community the hierarchy has a special responsibility to insure faithfulness to the Spirit, which Jesus has given to the church.

In reference to the personal, yet communal, aspect of faith, the *Catechism* says,

> Faith is a personal act—the free response of the human person to the initiative of God who reveals himself. But faith is not an isolated act. . . . The believer has received faith from others and should hand it on to others. . . . Each believer is thus a link in the great chain of believers.[42]

Shifting Perspectives

Pre-Vatican II Catholicism cast the Catholic story within the parameters of the *institutional* church, which clearly spelled out a Catholic's identity as a member of the one, true church. Catholics went to Mass each Sunday, confessed their sins to a

[42] *Catechism of the Catholic Church,* #166.

priest frequently, abstained from meat on Fridays, and knew the teachings of the *Baltimore Catechism*.

The church, through its many educational endeavors, taught the content of the Catholic message. Often, studying and reading the Scriptures privately was discouraged. The church told its members what it meant to be human, Christian, and Catholic. Catholics knew their story and accepted it.

At Vatican II, the Catholic story was recast within the context of the church as a *community*. As this happened, the roles of the laity, hierarchy, priests, and religious shifted focus. So did *interpretations* of the content of the Catholic Christian message.

The Catholic community gained new insights about God's presence in nature, people, and other religions at the same time that Catholic biblical, doctrinal, moral, and pastoral theology changed perspectives. Renewed appreciation of Scripture encouraged Catholics to apply the biblical message to their lives. They learned that Jesus proclaimed the reign (kingdom) of God and that he invited them to live his message of God's reign in their families, work situations, parishes, and dioceses. In the more open church that emerged, many pre-Vatican II practices changed and many theological and pastoral perspectives were refocused, but the basic beliefs of Catholicism remained.

The *Catechism* must be situated within the post-Vatican II Catholic Church. It will not bring immediate clarity to all doctrinal content and moral teachings, but it will help solidify basic beliefs and practices, clarify church teaching, and encourage Catholics to stress basic beliefs. It cannot be seen, however, as the final word on everything. In fact, all past catechisms have been marked by a limited effectiveness because each catechism is time bound, reflecting particular historical circumstances. If the *Catechism* had been written shortly after Vatican II, its emphasis would have been different. If a new catechism is written in twenty years, its focus will be different.

Catholic identity involves more than learning essential church teachings, for identity involves many aspects of church life. Learning Catholic teachings can contribute only so much to reestablish this identity.

How to use the *Catechism* effectively presents a challenge and a consolation to religious educators. The challenge centers around the overall health of the Catholic story as it is found in dioceses, parishes, and families. The quality of this health will determine the long-range effectiveness of the *Catechism*. The consolation rests in seeing that successful resolution of catechetical problems will depend on the combined efforts of parents, church leaders, and parishioners. Only together can the Catholic community revitalize the Catholic story by fulfilling its obligation to share Jesus' message at home, work, and parish.

The *Catechism of the Catholic Church* gives Catholics the opportunity to refocus catechesis, but it will be only as effective as the church's ability to cope with basic church issues today.

Beyond Facts and Memorization

Teaching the basic truths of Catholicism is an important aspect of the Catholic story. For this reason, early Christian churches formulated beliefs and creeds. The Acts of the Apostles recounts Peter's testimony on Pentecost, spelling out core Christian beliefs:

> Jesus the Nazarene was a man commended to you by God by the miracles and portents and signs that God worked through him when he was among you, as you all know. This man, who was put into your power by the deliberate intention and foreknowledge of God, you took and had crucified by men outside of the Law. You killed him, but God raised him to life. . . . Now raised to the heights by God's right hand, he has received from the Father the Holy Spirit, who was promised, and what you see and hear is the outpouring of that Spirit.[43]

---

[43] Acts 2:22–33.

To clarify the Jesus story, Christian Scriptures recounted foundational Christian beliefs, while church councils, liturgical formulae, creeds, popes, bishops, and theologians clarified these beliefs. The *Catechism of the Catholic Church* attempts to do the same thing for this generation.

In this clarification process, cultures and languages affect the attitudes and images that people use to express foundational beliefs. Hence, the intellectualization of beliefs in creed, code, or theological formulae is not the whole picture. Rational expressions of belief, in themselves, cannot establish Catholic identity, for identity happens in the interplay of the Christian story, its ritualization, the faith response of Christians ,and formulations of belief (content). The following schema illustrates this interplay:[44]

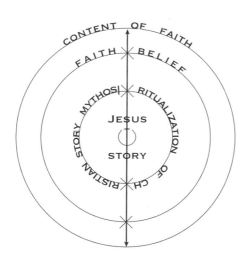

----

[44] This diagram is not intended to suggest that there is a sharp distinction between the dynamics operative in each of these sectors. There is overlap in each sector. For example, "faith" (third circle) is present as the "mythos/ rituals" develop. The "content" of Christian belief (final circle) also is present in each of the previous circles.

The *inner core* of the Catholic story begins with Jesus. From his life and teachings all Christian traditions emerged. As the *Catechism* says,

> "At the heart of catechesis we find, in essence, a Person, the Person of Jesus of Nazareth, the only Son from the Father . . . who suffered and died for us and who now, after rising, is living with us forever." [45]

The *second* circle describes the interplay between the Christian story and its ritualization in life and worship. This story, rooted in Jesus, emerges from the collective, fundamental attitudes of Catholics (the mythos) developed over the centuries.[46] These attitudes are lived out and celebrated in ritual activities, such as baptism, Eucharist, and various expressions of the Catholic lifestyle.

The *third* circle implies that communal or personal faith emerges from the interplay of the Catholic story and its ritualization, as the community and individuals say "yes" to this story. Simply put, faith is a person's or group's saying "amen" to the Catholic story. This "ownership" of the story, in turn, moves a person or community to live according to the dictates of the story.

The *fourth* circle indicates that creeds, codes, or other formulations of belief rest on and emerge from the deeper dynamics that root the Catholic story and its ritualization. Intellectualization of the fundamental core of community belief (content statements) is a part of, and a valuable way to clarify, the Catholic story, but in itself it never establishes identity. Identity is forged in the interplay of the story and its ritualization in the faith history and experience of a community of believers. The content of the story can express only what happens on a deeper level and is always an inadequate

---

[45] *Catechism of the Catholic Church,* #426, quoting CT5.

[46] A fuller explanation of "mythos" is found on p. 53.

approximation of the mystery that roots the relationship of God and the Catholic community.

The *Catechism* is most properly situated within the fourth circle. It clarifies essential Catholic belief and establishes benchmarks, reflecting key elements of the Catholic belief system.

Elements contained in each circle are essential in passing on the faith. The deepest dimensions of conversion begin with the inner circles. Although formulae of faith (the creed or specific teachings) can trigger new awareness, leading to deeper dimensions of conversion, in themselves they do not cause conversion.

Since Vatican II, the focus of the Catholic story and its ritualization are still shifting. In this context, the ramifications for religious educators of the four-circle diagram are obvious. These ramifications center around the basic premise that teaching the fourth circle (creeds, codes, or other formulations of belief) without rooting such teachings in elements contained in the other three circles makes little sense as far as conversion is concerned. It may have some value when studying *about* religious beliefs, but little value when the intention is to elicit or deepen faith.

If, however, the teachings in the fourth circle are connected to the center through the arrows describing the complete process, such teachings can have immense value. They solidify and clarify what a person may only have vaguely perceived up to this point. For example, a young person may have experienced family love and parish faith rituals centering around Jesus, but the meaning of such experiences may be vague in his or her life until the individual learns about Jesus, the church, and the reasons why Catholics believe as they do. It is precisely this element of clarification that often has been missing in post-Vatican II catechesis. Consequently, many youth and adults may know in a vague way what it means to be Catholic but have little knowledge to substantiate why or what they believe.

Catholics are encouraged to learn the basic, unchanging teachings of the church and those which, while not defined, are certain, Catholic beliefs. Centering Catholic teachings in Jesus' story also gives Catholics a clearer perception of what is essential to their belief and what is more peripheral. An important criterion that the church has used traditionally to discern the central elements of Catholic Christian belief is how a particular belief relates to the centrality of Jesus' story. For example, belief in devotion to the saints is important, but is not nearly as central to the message of the Gospels as is Jesus' teaching on social justice.

For the *Catechism* to bear fruit, it needs to be situated within the perspectives developed in the models of the four circles, described above. With these in mind, the following ramifications seem obvious.

First, the *Catechism* challenges bishops, pastors, parents, and religion teachers to concentrate on teaching the basics of the faith, while acknowledging that more is required to reestablish Catholic identity. Teaching Catholics the content of faith, in itself, will not make active Catholics or resolve faith doubts.

Second, the *Catechism* invites catechists to refocus on basic teachings within the faith context described in the four circles. After Vatican II, teaching the basics of the faith sometimes was minimized. Ignorance of the fundamentals of faith had serious consequences, illustrated by the numbers of adult Catholics, educated in Catholic schools or parishes, who are almost religiously illiterate. The *Catechism* offers the opportunity to change this situation.

While the Catholic story goes beyond facts, learning them plays a vital piece in Catholic identity. Catholics learn who they are through living witnesses of faith and by learning what Jesus and the church teach. This requires the ability to understand and express basic elements of the faith. In the past, this happened through memorizing the catechism. Today, new ways must be devised to make it happen.

With the publication of the *Catechism of the Catholic Church*, it is also time to ask, "What about memorization?"

Memory is a great gift of God. People memorize facts in history, science, and mathematics. Why not religion? Catholics need to know prayers, Scripture, creed, and basic teachings. Short formulae of faith are valuable ways to clarify basic Catholic teaching. In saying this, however, it is important to remember that memorization alone does not produce faith that is "living, conscious and active."[47]

Returning to the catechism memorization method is not the answer. This method was used before Vatican II, when it was believed that the best way to learn the clear-cut message that the church taught was to memorize it.

Seen from a present-day perspective, this method has its limitations. It does not foster adult education, Scripture is not emphasized, and short answers to complex questions often leave important issues unlearned.

Today, effective catechetical methods incorporate other aspects of catechesis developed since Vatican II.[48] In this context, however, certain benchmarks of Catholicism, learned by memorizing short formulae of belief, can provide Catholics a stability similar to the stability afforded to Protestants who memorize biblical passages as indicators of their beliefs and practices. The latter practice need not be confined to Protestants. Catholics can memorize key passages from Scriptures and basic church teachings to help ground their Catholic faith.

While advocating some memorization, another question needs to be asked: "Memorization for the sake of what?" Memorization or learning facts is necessary because memory helps root a person's identity and put together the "big picture." For Catholics, this big picture centers around knowledge of the faith tradition, which is essential for understanding the wisdom and meaning of Catholicism and for critical reflection upon the Catholic faith or particular aspects of belief and practice.

---

[47] "Bishops' Pastoral Office in the Church," *The Documents of Vatican II*, #14.
[48] See Chapter Four.

The ability to reflect on a person's faith and on the questions being raised at this point in history is extremely important, because in an open society Catholic adults are called upon frequently to assess situations and make moral decisions in the light of the beliefs and traditions of their faith. Memorization which leads to an isolated outcome is not the issue; rather, the goal is memorization as a tool to provide the general knowledge to help Catholics face the many challenges of today's world.

Memorizing key biblical passages also enhances the understanding of God's Word. This can be valuable in a person's devotional life, for Scripture provides a rich source of meditation, relating God's Word with everyday experiences.

Catholics need to consider the suggestion of memorizing key biblical passages in light of a basic historical-critical approach to Scripture, in which the development of Scripture is understood, and in which the memorizer can place the passage in the larger context of the book/letter/gospel out of which it has come. Otherwise, the outcome may become a proof-texting approach to Scripture, which the church has struggled to avoid and which many Catholics and Protestants find unacceptable.

II. *CATECHISM OF THE CATHOLIC CHURCH,* CONVERSION AND METHODS

The *Catechism* speaks of adaptations, necessary to relate the message of the *Catechism* to "differences of culture, age, spiritual maturity, and social and ecclesial condition among all those to whom it is addressed."[49] To help users of the *Catechism* appreciate the dynamics involved in such adaptations, this section considers two chief areas: (1) the social dynamics operative in any group, developed under the aspects of mythos (myth), ritual, and symbol; and (2) the relationship of conversion and methods.

---

[49] *Catechism of the Catholic Church,* #24; also see footnote 30.

Mythos (Myth), Ritual, Faith, Ethos/Ethics, and Symbol

The interrelationships in any society, group, family, parish, or social gathering involve certain dynamics which can be classified under the headings of mythos, myth, ritual, symbol, faith, ethos/ethics, and models. These interrelationships may be viewed schematically in the following way:

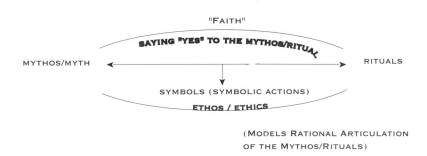

(MODELS RATIONAL ARTICULATION
OF THE MYTHOS/RITUALS)

The dynamics operative in this schema influence the conversion process. Consequently, they impact upon effective use of the *Catechism*, for the *Catechism* must be adapted to the cultural contexts of those being catechized. Such adaptation is influenced by the dynamics present in the group itself. The elements in this schema are described below to help the reader better understand their implications when using the *Catechism*. Such implications are developed, using the terms of this schema, in succeeding pages of this book.

Mythos refers to the fundamental attitude of a family, church, business office, society, or any other group.[50] This attitude is very real for the group involved, and usually operates below the

---

[50] It must be noted that this book uses the terms "mythos" and "myth" in their technical sense. This differs from their common meaning and popular use, where "mythos" and "myth" often refer to something unreal or to a fictional representation of something that may or may not ever have happened.

level of consciousness. Each group, small or large, has one or
many mythos, which establish the basic groundwork for human
interaction within and beyond the group.

Mythos operates on a societal and personal level. A societal mythos influences all members of a particular group, while
a personal mythos influences an individual's attitudes, beliefs,
and ways of acting.

Before Vatican II, the Catholic mythos pictured
Catholicism as the one, true church and forbade inter-Christian
worship with other religious denominations. Mass was in Latin,
celebrated exactly the same way everywhere, with little regard
for people's own languages or customs. The Catholic mythos
emphasized Jesus' divinity, encouraged regular confessions,
mandated Friday abstinence, and practiced many devotions.
God's holiness and human unworthiness were stressed, as was
faithful adherence to church teachings. The pope, bishops,
priests, brothers, and sisters ministered in the church's name,
while lay people followed church leaders. This Catholic mythos
reflected the church's isolation from the world and other
churches. Today, this closed worldview has changed; so have its
mythos, rituals, and teachings.

The content and use of the *Baltimore Catechism* reflected the pre-Vatican II mythos. Its teachings and application were
consistent with the Catholic mythos of the times.

After Vatican II, the Catholic mythos shifted. This shift
altered the focus of the message and the need to apply it to
various personal, family, parish, and diocesan circumstances.
Consequently, catechesis changed focus to correspond with this
changing Catholic mythos. The *Catechism of the Catholic
Church* also reflects this shift.

The patterns, or ways of relating, that flow from a certain mythos are called *mythical patterns*. These include a group's
distinctive ways of looking at the world, other people, and its
own members. Thus, for example, when Vatican II set the stage
for changing perspectives on the laity, the mythical patterns
that formerly limited parish catechesis almost exclusively to

priests and religious changed. Such changes were in line with changing perspectives on the content of Catholicism and various methods that developed.

A group's mythos shapes its *myths*.[51] A myth attempts to express some aspect of a group's mythos. The most basic way this happens is through the group's story or stories. The myth can be conveyed orally, in writing, or through technology. It always expresses fundamental notions contained in the mythos.

In Jesus' time, mythos was expressed primarily through oral communication, the dominant communication mode of his time. Jesus revealed orally the fundamental core of the Christian mythos, namely, the reign of God, but he wrote nothing that has come down to us. Likewise, after his death, the Christian mythos first was handed down orally. Only subsequently was it written down.

When Western civilization became more and more dependent on writing, mythical expressions of the story shifted to the print medium. This was accentuated in the sixteenth century when Gutenberg developed the printing press. Today, the predominant mode of communication is increasingly tech-nological (i.e., television, computers, video). Mass media, especially television, exert significant influence on the modern myth.

The influence of technology on the contemporary cul-tural mythos points to the significance of media in applying the content of the *Catechism* to various catechetical contexts.

Ritual is a patterned acting-out of a mythos that a group has made its own. In other words, rituals act out the mythos of each family, church, neighborhood, country, school, or other group.

The rituals of the pre-Vatican II Catholic Church were consistent with its mythos. This changed at Vatican II. Among other things, the changing Catholic mythos encouraged liturgi-cal celebrations in people's own languages. It also affected other

---

[51] See footnote 50.

church rituals, such as devotions, fasting, memorizing catechism answers, parish style, religious garb, and lay involvement in parishes. Changing ritual patterns influenced parish reorganization, hospitality, priest-laity relationships, church authority, clerical and religious lifestyle, liturgical effectiveness, and catechetical methodology.

The *Catechism of the Catholic Church* reflects these ritualistic changes. They are evident especially in sections of the *Catechism* that deal with the church's sacramental, devotional, and prayer life. Such changes influenced both the content of catechetical materials and its integration with the liturgical life of those being catechized.

Symbols can be actions, words, or things. They may be natural symbols, like water or fire, or culturally produced symbols, like a flag or wedding ring. Symbols include a handshake, kiss, picture, crucifix, baptismal water, or statue.

Every symbol has meaning in relation to the mythos out of which it emerges. For example, I have two pictures, the one of a five-year-old girl sitting on an antique chair, the other of a young married couple. Both pictures are about eighty years old. One is a powerful symbol for me, the other is not. The first is a symbol because it is a picture of my mother as a child. Its power comes from our close relationship over a lifetime. The second is a picture I bought at an auction because I liked the frame.

To appreciate any religious symbol, like baptismal water, people need to understand the Catholic mythos surrounding Jesus, church, and baptism into Christ. Likewise, appreciation of the Eucharist is influenced by people's mythos of Jesus, real presence, and Christian community. For a believer, the Eucharist is the Lord; for an unbeliever, it is a piece of bread.

After Vatican II, many Catholic symbols, like confession, Eucharist, crucifix, rosary, and statues, shifted focus. Such changing perspectives are reflected in the orientation of the *Catechism,* as well as in contemporary catechesis.

Faith is saying "yes" to an individual's or group's mythos and rituals. Thus, for example, when mutual trust develops between two friends, their faith enables them to say, "I believe you," even when the evidence may indicate otherwise. Every act of faith involves saying "yes" to someone's or some group's mythos and rituals.

In a religious context, Catholic faith is saying "yes" to the Catholic mythos and rituals. Before Vatican II, this "yes" was couched in the Catholic world of the time. In one way, this was faith more in the church than in Jesus Christ. After Vatican II, the faith of many Catholics wavered as their mythos and rituals changed. Today, the church encourages Catholics to see the church community, not as an end in itself, but as an important means to encounter the Risen Christ.

Ethos refers to a particular moral orientation or spirit embodied in a community or group. It includes acceptable and unacceptable norms of conduct. These flow from a group's mythos and rituals, which set the standard for morality. Such norms may vary from group to group, nation to nation, individual to individual. United States culture has certain acceptable standards of conduct, which may or may not conform to those of another country or the church. From a religious perspective, various denominations teach their community's ethos in their interpretation of right and wrong. *Ethics* refers to a systematic study of the moral orientation, principles, and practices flowing from a particular ethos. Ethics involves rational analysis and operates within the context of models. The *Catechism of the Catholic Church* clarifies today's Catholic ethos/ethics in light of the teachings of Vatican II.

Models are rational constructs which attempt to put order into human life and thought. They describe in rational language what is happening in a group's mythos and rituals.

Scientists develop models of the universe. Sociologists use them to explain group behavior. Theologians employ them to clarify religious thinking. In short, models identify essential elements of a particular mythos, natural system, or human enterprise.

Before Vatican II, the generally accepted model of the church was a "perfect society." Today, Catholics consider the church more in terms of a community based on discipleship, proclamation of the Word, sacrament and service. The institution serves to facilitate the church as a community of believers. These models are used to clarify the contemporary Catholic mythos and rituals. [52]

The *Catechism of the Catholic Church* fits into the category of a model. It is a model that puts into rational language the basic teachings of the post-Vatican II Catholic Church.

Understanding the basic dynamics operative on the level of mythos, myth, ritual, symbol, faith, ethos/ethics, and models helps catechists, parents, and church ministers appreciate the dynamics underlying any successful use of the *Catechism*. It also helps them understand more fully the meaning of conversion and its relationship to methodology.

Conversion and Methods[53]

The goal of all catechesis is conversion. Keeping this in mind helps catechists appreciate better the relationship of the content of the *Catechism* to the broader perspectives involved in a person's coming to faith.

Conversion is a significant deepening, recentering, or refocusing of life patterns, energy, loyalties, attitudes, and values. This process can be individual or communal. It lasts a lifetime and may be gradual or intensified because of a traumatic experience.

In simplest terms, conversion means "seeing in a new way." For example, conversion may happen after a child's

---

[52] See Avery Dulles, *Models of the Church*.

[53] Parts of this section are taken from my article "Facilitating Conversion Processes" in *Christian Adulthood* (USCC, 1987), pp. 3–15.

serious illness, when a parent sees in a new way the priority of family life over making money.

Religious conversion is a specific type of conversion that centers around discovering a deeper meaning in life. Christian conversion involves seeing life's meaning in light of Jesus.

Religious conversion begins with God seeking a person. This divine quest emerges from within an individual, is revealed through community, and clarified through reflection. Because God's revealing presence embraces all dimensions of life, the entire world invites humans to conversion, which goes beyond specific church activities.

Conversion: Modes of God's Revealing Presence

God's revealing presence happens in different ways. Human awareness is like the top of a wave, receiving direction and impetus from deep within. Although each person is whole and undivided, reason can identify three ways or modes that God's sacramental world discloses links between people, God, and community. These modes refer to one's innermost being (Core Mode), one's participation in community (Community Mode), and one's conscious consideration or rational approach (Consideration Mode).[54]

Like a swirl or spiral, the dynamic involved in this process of God's self-revelation moves from an intimate depth within a person, where God energizes the human spirit (Core), to the outer limit of human consciousness (Consideration). The entire movement flows through group response (Community), where family, friends, parish, work, and culture help shape attitudes and values. This can be pictured schematically in the following diagram.

---

[54] These modes are not meant to describe completely the conversion process but, rather, to illustrate certain dimensions of God's revealing presence manifested through the sacramental world. These modes are rational constructs that do not exist as such; rather, they are used to point to facets of a person's life.

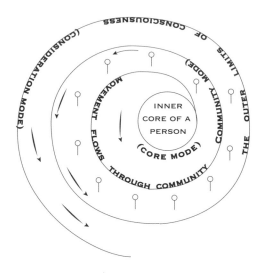

Core Mode

The Core Mode refers to the deepest dimensions of the person, from which human energy ultimately emerges and where primal urges move people to search for meaning. This wellspring, continually energized by God, roots life's meaning system. Here, God is met in the form of spiritual energy, creative awareness, and intuitive insight. From this source, questions such as "Who am I?" and "Why was I born?" emerge. Here, the sacred explodes from the ground of creation, as God grasps people and invites them to say, "Amen!" Often, this encounter with God happens in prayer.

The *Catechism of the Catholic Church* reflects the reality of this basic dimension of the human person in saying,

> The desire for God is written in the human heart. . . Created in God's image and called to know and love him, the person who seeks God discovers certain ways of coming to know him. . . . The soul, the "seed of eternity we bear in ourselves, irreducible to the merely material," can have its origin only in God. [55]

---

[55] *Catechism of the Catholic Church*, #27, 31, and 33, quoting GS 18 #1; 14 #2.

Questions emerge spontaneously from the Core Mode and cannot be programmed, as people respond to the unpredictable invitations of a radically free God. This mode makes it possible for people of different religious beliefs to identify with the meaning of what is said when someone shares a deep personal experience. (This happened at a Hindu-Christian prayer service. When a Christian read a gospel account of Jesus' agony and death, the Hindu holy men wept, feeling deeply the universal meaning of sin, suffering and death.)[56]

The Core Mode moves humans instinctively to search for meaning beyond functional everyday activities, like making money or going to the store. It roots their deeper need for happiness, joy, and peace. In using the *Catechism*, catechists need to connect with this level in those being catechized, so that the lessons taught touch their basic human needs.

Community Mode

The Community Mode describes the situations in which humans interact on a deep level (e.g., family, friends, work, church). In community, people are influenced by the way their particular mythos and rituals interpret the energies flowing from the Core Mode. So, for example, a mother tells her son that she forgives him by putting her arms around him, while an older Native American asks for healing by going into the tribe's religious sweat lodge. Cultural, historical, and confessional myths and beliefs affect the shape and focus of these deep core energies.

Because God chooses when, where, and how to reveal "the holy," mystery grounds community. Hence, no matter how much a community supports an individual in a time of grief, the "why?" surrounding suffering and death will remain.

On the other hand, since God is revealed in time, the community formed from faith in a given revelation is experiential and historical. Consequently, believing Christians respond

---

[56] See the event that took place in Madras, India.

to Jesus' story both from a core depth common to all religious people and from their particular belief that Jesus reveals God's healing, forgiveness, and love.

Community is central to God's revealing presence and always conditions it. Thus, knowledge of and sensitivity to people's living situations are important for facilitating individual and communal conversion. When dealing with troubled children in a catechetical session, for example, the degree to which a catechist can help them take positive steps forward often depends on whether or not the catechist appreciates what is actually happening in their lives.

Since the Core Mode is linked with community action, it helps to look at the basic energies operative in community. The mythical and ritual patterns that keep a love relationship strong, solidify family ties, or insure a healthy catechetical environment go deeper than rational planning. Whenever people come together, complex dynamics interrelate. At times, this is positive, resulting in love, cooperation, and trust. But the opposite can also occur, namely, jealousy, bickering, and destructive competition.

Consideration Mode

The Consideration Mode refers to situations in which humans employ rational thought to plan, construct projects, analyze results, or rationally reflect on their actions and beliefs. This mode is understood to mean the level of human knowledge that includes intellectual discourse, development of models in business or theology, abstract formulae of faith, rational analyses of situations, clarifications in business, theological or philosophical statements, and the whole range of human intellectual activities. It is not to be dichotomized from the rest of the person, and always is influenced by other aspects of one's life, such as culture, emotional state, or previous presuppositions.

The intellect or reason is a great gift from God which distinguishes humans from the rest of known creation. As such, reason plays a vital part in catechesis, for the intellect enables them to know God, learn the church's traditions, and profess faith. Catechists need to feed the mind as well as soothe the heart in order to minister to the whole person.

The Consideration Mode, which is made possible because of human intellectual powers, operates within the complex maze of human feelings and attitudes by bringing to bear human rational powers on a situation, problem, or issue. From a religious viewpoint, this enables people to formulate doctrines and creeds, as well as to understand the motives for actions. This mode allows people to learn about the faith, pass religious records on to the next generation, interpret historical events, and develop models in theology.

The Consideration Mode is the place where the *Catechism of the Catholic Church* most properly fits. It is a rational formulation of the basic belief and practices of the Catholic Church. For it to be used effectively, however, it needs to be related in some way to the mythos and rituals of those being catechized.

While energies flow among the Core, Community, and Consideration Modes, the latter mode is significant in personal conversion to the degree that it illuminates the other modes and meshes with them. Consequently, it is imperative that the *Catechism* is used in such a way that its teachings relate to the community needs of those being catechized and speak to the deepest energies and meaning questions flowing from the Core Mode. Otherwise, the *Catechism* becomes an exercise in intellectual acumen and never touches the level of mystery, where real conversion happens. For example, a religion teacher or catechist might insist that a student or catechumen learn an abstract definition of "grace" (Consideration Mode) without integrating such teaching into a wider biblical or pastoral context, or without showing its relationship to the human or church community (Community Mode), or without relating it to the student's or catechumen's life (Core Mode).

The aim of all conversion efforts, toward which the *Catechism* is geared, is to touch the dimension of mystery at the

Core Mode, which is more basic than the intellectual conversion of the Consideration Mode.

These three modes, focusing the divine energies that
root conversion, spiral out from deep within a person, through
community, to consciousness, only to return again to their
source in a constant vortex of human awareness.

Another way to consider these modes is to compare
their relationship to the flame of a candle. The hottest part of a
candle flame, the pure blue fire at the center of the flame, can
be compared to the Core Mode. This is the hottest energy
source. Away from the center, red streaks appear, and these
become more apparent at the outer limits of the flame. These
red streaks are indications of the imperfect burning of the oxygen. The outer limits of the flame, removed from the core, are
not as hot, and are comparable to the Consideration Mode.
Without oxygen, the flame would soon burn out. The purity of
the oxygen influences the intensity of the fire. The oxygen is
comparable to the Community Mode, necessary to maintain the
Core and Consideration Modes. This is illustrated in the following way:

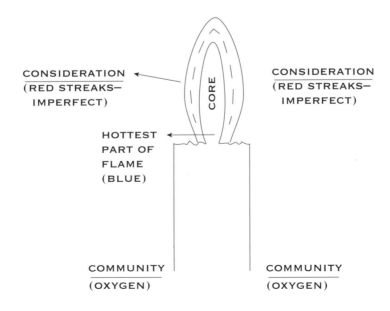

CONSIDERATION
(RED STREAKS—
IMPERFECT)

CORE

CONSIDERATION
(RED STREAKS—
IMPERFECT)

HOTTEST
PART OF
FLAME
(BLUE)

COMMUNITY
(OXYGEN)

COMMUNITY
(OXYGEN)

From the illustration's considerations, it becomes apparent that the Consideration Mode, which plays a vital part in human growth and awareness, has limits. In itself, it often fails to touch the core of human becoming. This appreciation is paramount when using the *Catechism*, for if basic church teaching is not nourished in community (the oxygen), and rooted in the Core Mode (the hot blue core), its results may not touch people's deep needs.

Catechesis: Conversion, Methods, and Facilitating Conversion Processes

Catechesis is an important part of a person's coming to faith (conversion), which involves ongoing cooperation with God's grace.[57] Since catechists help people respond to God's grace by *teaching* them the basics of their faith, it can never be forgotten that catechesis is primarily about instruction. Again, this focus on instruction illustrates the importance of knowledge in a person's coming to faith and living the faith.

An important aspect of instruction is teaching the basic facts of the Catholic faith, the knowledge of which can assist a person in his or her conversion. Such conversion does not happen automatically, however, when a person memorizes facts. Consequently, the primary goal of catechesis is to help facilitate a person's conversion, not to impart facts for their own sake.

To help facilitate a person's conversion, effective methods need to be used. This section clarifies the relationship between conversion and methods to help facilitate it.

Conversion

If a person shifts his or her way of thinking and acting in light of new insights coming as the result of a retreat, a painful experience, or a joyous event, he or she can be said to have experienced a new level of conversion. If this happens within a faith context, the person is bound to perceive his or her life

---

[57] See Pope John Paul II, *Catechesi Tradendae*, #18.

more deeply in terms of purpose, relationship with God/
Jesus/Church, and responsibilities to other persons and the
planet.

Often, when conversion happens, four elements are present: (1) personal experience; (2) allowing that experience to
encounter a broader environment, including the larger Catholic
Christian story; (3) illuminating the experience through the
encounter and grounding it in prayer, Scripture, church teaching, and history; and (4) responding to the insights gleaned in
acts of prayer, service, and celebration. These four elements
need not flow sequentially nor be present at all times, and each
element can happen whether one is alone or with others.

Community is central to conversion. An individual
"becomes" in community. Martin Buber once said that it takes
a "Thou" to create an "I."[58] In community, God is disclosed; in
community, a person is supported and encouraged; in community, personal meaning is most fully revealed. Because
community influence differs with each person, individuals
interpret a communal mythos differently. Acknowledging unity
in diversity, yet diversity in community, reinforces the need for
flexible methods, as people move across the boundaries of age,
group, parish, and country. While Core Mode questions are
the same for all people, the mythical responses in community
vary greatly due to local circumstances and group differences.
Although it requires community, personal conversion is always
an individual search and ought to be facilitated as such.

Since conversion differs from person to person, a person
may need time alone to enhance conversion. Later, he or she
may prefer limited group interaction or more intense dialogue.
A person's mythos significantly influences the most appropriate
method for that individual.

---

[58] See Martin Buber, *I and Thou* (New York: Charles Scribner's Sons, 1970).

Methods to Help Facilitate Conversion

Many methods aimed at facilitating conversion have developed in the Catholic Church since Vatican II. These include: the Rite of Christian Initiation of Adults, RENEW, Christ Renews His Parish, Marriage Encounter, and Cursillo. The goal of all these methods is conversion, namely, helping a person or community to say "yes" to Jesus and his message. This section addresses such methods by considering them in relation to conversion.

The term "method," used here in a broad sense, refers to any process intended to help facilitate individual or communal conversion. Every method used to facilitate conversion (e.g., at home, Catholic school ministry, catechetical sessions, RCIA, youth ministry) includes a learning process, involving a person and an environment. The person brings to the environment a certain mythos resulting from past experiences. The environment, having its own mythos, can be private space (e.g., sitting alone in church, a retreat, solitary meditation, or the privacy of one's room) or group interaction (classroom, family, friends, or church events). The interaction between the person and the environment usually influences the effectiveness of the efforts to facilitate conversion.

A distinction must be made between conversion itself, which always happens in a person or group, and methods used to facilitate it. The former is an end; the latter are means. The ultimate purpose of individual or communal conversion is deeper union with God, achieved through relationships with the sacramental world.

Any systematic attempt to help facilitate conversion must consider four factors: persons, context, method (including content material), and facilitator. The method chosen in any systematic or structured conversion situation (e.g., RCIA, catechetical session, parish school of religion, Catholic school religion class, or adult formation sessions) should address these factors in light of the mythos involved.[59] Thus, to facilitate conversion is to acknowledge the mythos out of which people respond.

Hence, methods will vary according to culture, situation, and persons. Just as no one creed or intellectual formula expresses Catholic belief adequately for all times, neither does any single method best satisfy every person's or group's needs.

Since conversion is the process of gaining new insights into life's meaning, efforts to help facilitate conversion need to center around shared meaning. In a sacramental world, the search for meaning always returns to the Core Mode, where God intimately addresses people. One's relationship with God roots all shared meaning, is the goal of conversion, and is enhanced by dialogue.

Hence, the common center toward which all conversion aims and on which all methodologies focus is every person's search for meaning. In this search for meaning, a highly individualized, scientific, technological, and pragmatic outlook can easily allow people to neglect the Core Mode by stressing a functional world view that implies that anything not measurable is second-rate or meaningless. In this context, methods to facilitate conversion must move beyond the functional to address ultimate questions.

The world within which God invites people to new levels of meaning includes three chief disclosure points: family, ecclesial community, and personal activities (work, prayer, play, friends, community involvement, nature). Facilitating conversion means acknowledging these disclosure points in culture, seeing God's presence there, and developing methodology consistent with a heterogeneous mix of learners.

---

[59] During the 1980s, "Shared Christian Practice," a method popularized by Thomas H. Groome, was popular among many catechists. This method significantly influenced catechesis during this period. See Thomas H. Groome, *Christian Religious Education* (San Francisco: Harper and Row, 1980).

Catechesis: Facilitating Conversion and the *Catechism of the Catholic Church*

Selecting an effective catechetical method demands sensitivity to people's mythical perspective. In one instance, it may be wise to begin a group session with dialogue; in another, with a didactic approach, gradually moving to a collaborative one. No one method works at all times with all people. All methods, however, need to be rooted in prayer.

Because the individual's mythos significantly influences the conversion process, methods and content materials should aim at touching people's mythical perspectives. If, for example, a child is struggling with the divorce of his or her parents, this mythical perspective in the child's life needs to be considered when planning how best to teach the Catholic approach to the indissolubility of marriage, or to reflect the teachings of the *Catechism* that speak to this issue. People's divergent mythical attitudes also indicate why any systematic approach to catechesis needs to move beyond the Community and Consideration Modes to the Core Mode.

Central to the use of a catechetical method is recognition that people are at different levels of conversion. Some may be questioning God's existence; others, Jesus' divinity; still others, the church. Those in the first category will be influenced little by church rules and obligations. Wise catechists need to begin where people are. Otherwise, catechesis will have minimal impact.

Effective catechesis also demands accommodating a method to a catechist's knowledge, skills, style, and disposition. For example, one catechist may begin a catechetical session with some input and then draw implications from the students. Another may begin with a sharing session and introduce the content within the group's response.

Catechetical methods may vary from lectures to dialogue. Although different methods can be used at different phases of the conversion process, any effective method always takes into account the mythos of those being catechized, the environment, and the catechist's skills.

Catechists learn from Jesus himself that there is no one best method to facilitate conversion. He used many methods to bring people to God's Word. Some of these methods included: teaching the Law, discussing God with the disciples, preaching in the synagogue or on the Mount, telling stories in parables, working miracles, showing compassion, standing up for the truth, and forgiving sinners. The *Catechism*, quoting the *Roman Catechism*, reflects the importance of employing varying methods when it says,

> Above all, teachers must not imagine that a single kind of soul has been entrusted to them, and that consequently it is lawful to teach and form equally all the faithful in true piety with one and the same method! Let them realize that some are in Christ as newborn babes, others as adolescents, and still others as adults in full command of their power. . . .[60]

Catechists help those being catechized to apply basic church teaching to their lives. Here is where methods come into play. No sure-fire method exists to make this happen. During the past twenty-five years, various methods took their turn in popularity in the Catholic community. Each made valuable contributions. At the present time, the RCIA enjoys great success in bringing people to conversion. Let it be noted, however, that the RCIA is a method, not conversion itself. As such, it admits of exceptions. Although parishes normally use it to initiate new Catholics, situations arise when a different method may be required. To canonize one method to the exclusion of all others is to straight-jacket the Holy Spirit. No single method suffices for all circumstances.

The same is true for the *Catechism*. The *Dossier* makes this clear by stating that "pedagogical and methodological/didactic applications are avoided in so far as these vary according to

---

[60] *Catechism of the Catholic Church*, #24, quoting the *Roman Catechism*.

those to whom the catechesis is directed and to cultural contexts."[61]

The *Catechism* will help bring people to a greater appreciation of the Catholic story and its personal implications if its insights are used in a method that makes sense to the person(s) being catechized. In other words, it is necessary that such a method touch the Core Mode, speak to people's lives, help them discover God within their experiences, and reflect upon their lives in light of the Christian story so as to move toward some type of lifestyle response, such as repentance, prayer, social action, or charity.

Using the *Catechism*, or materials derived from it, is one way to present basic church teaching. Hopefully, a catechist will use such materials to help those being catechized relate basic church teaching to the deep energies of the Core Mode. An important question, then, becomes: "Does the method being used help conversion happen in a significant way?" Answering this question affirmatively is more important than insisting that everyone follow the same catechetical method.

Recognizing the distinction between conversion and various methods to facilitate it is critical. For example, the RCIA advocates a flexible process, accommodated to personal needs and local circumstances. Within it, there is no one best way to catechize. An experience illustrates this point. An RCIA leader insisted that the only way to catechize is to use exclusively the Sunday Lectionary readings, saying, "No other books should be used." Who says so?

The origins of the catechumenate reveal different methods, developed in various churches (Rome, Jerusalem, Hippo, Constantinople, Milan), to prepare catechumens.[62] The above quoted statement absolutizes a method, which is only a means

---

[61] *Dossier*, p. 22.
[62] See Robert J. Hater, "Facilitating Conversion Processes," in *Christian Adulthood* (USCC, 1987), p. 11, fn. 11.

to help facilitate conversion. Lectionary-based catechesis may be useful, but in itself it is inadequate.

The same applies to the *Catechism of the Catholic Church*. The goal in using it is to help facilitate the ongoing conversion of those being catechized. How this is done is a question of method, which can vary greatly. When the distinction between conversion and method is overlooked, problems arise, especially if the *Catechism* itself, or one way of using it, is canonized.

Today's complex world invites Catholics to return prayerfully to the simple message of the Gospels and to catechize in a holistic way. This means recognizing people's diversity and being realistic about community. To proclaim "Good News," no one method is sufficient. Rather, catechists must respond to people's needs and look again at how Jesus taught— by sharing a message, telling a story, inviting people to come together to consider its consequences and to derive meaning from the mystery of God-among-us. Jesus gave this challenge to his first disciples; he also gives it to catechists today.

CHAPTER THREE

CHANGING CLIMATE
OF CATECHESIS IN LIGHT
OF CONTEMPORARY CULTURE

S o that (God's) call should resound throughout the world, Christ sent forth the apostles he had chosen, commissioning them to proclaim the gospel: "Go therefore and make disciples of all nations . . . and lo, I am with you always to the close of the age." Strengthened by this mission, the apostles "went forth and preached everywhere, while the Lord worked with them and confirmed the message by the signs that attended it."

Those who with God's help have welcomed Christ's call and freely responded to it are urged on by love of Christ to proclaim the Good News everywhere in the world. This treasure, received from the apostles, has been faithfully guarded by their successors. All Christ's faithful are called to hand it on from generation to generation, by professing the faith, by living it in fraternal sharing, and by celebrating it in liturgy and prayer.[63]

---

[63] *Catechism of the Catholic Church*, #2, and 3, quoting Matthew 28:10 and Mark 16:20.

The *Catechism of the Catholic Church* contains "the essential and fundamental content of Catholic faith and morals in a complete and summary way."[64] For its successful application to catechesis, catechists need to take into consideration people's cultural contexts. In speaking of this, the *Catechism* says,

> Such indispensable adaptations are the responsibility of particular catechisms and, even more, of those who instruct the faithful.[65]

For this to happen, catechists have to link the content of the *Catechism* with solid methodological procedures and to appreciate the cultural situation of those being catechized. To put the *Catechism* into better perspective, this chapter examines catechesis in light of significant cultural dynamics, United States culture, and the contemporary needs of people.

I. SIGNIFICANT CULTURAL DYNAMICS

Every culture weaves together life's ultimate and functional aspects. For example, ultimate aspects include showing love, expressing concern, praying, and celebrating. Functional aspects include working in an office, driving a truck, and cutting the grass. Both the ultimate and functional are necessary for a happy life, but often they are hard to balance. The schema on the following page illustrates key features of both aspects.

To clarify further this schema, it may be noted that the ultimate aspects of life include personal relationships, deep family dynamics, significant community involvement, subjective responses, play, prayer, love commitments, personal fulfillment, and altruism. It is the realm of mystery, which never can be fathomed completely by reason alone. It looks at the whole person and includes activities like art, religion, aesthetics, and philosophy. Put simply, the ultimate tends toward the end or purpose of life with its source in God.

---

[64] *Dossier*, p. 21.

[65] *Catechism of the Catholic Church*, #24.

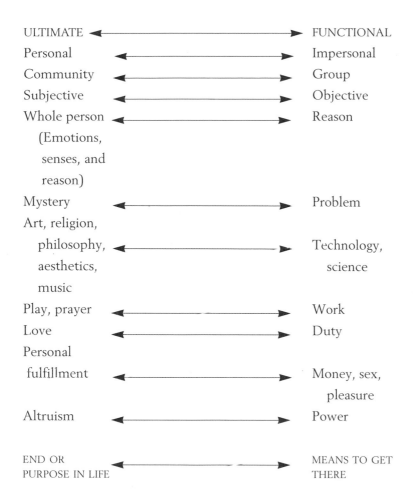

ULTIMATE ←————————————→ FUNCTIONAL

Personal ←————————————→ Impersonal

Community ←————————————→ Group

Subjective ←————————————→ Objective

Whole person ←————————————→ Reason
(Emotions,
senses, and
reason)

Mystery ←————————————→ Problem

Art, religion,
philosophy, ←————————————→ Technology,
aesthetics,   science
music

Play, prayer ←————————————→ Work

Love ←————————————→ Duty

Personal
fulfillment ←————————————→ Money, sex,
pleasure

Altruism ←————————————→ Power

END OR ←————————————→ MEANS TO GET
PURPOSE IN LIFE   THERE

On the other hand, functional aspects of life include impersonal activities or relationships, involvements with work associates or other groups, objective analyses of events, work, science, technology, making money, and fulfilling one's duty. It is the domain of reason and power and is concerned about problem solving. Put simply, it centers around the *means* used to achieve one's ultimate purpose in life.

Since the ultimate is associated with life's purpose, it is the most basic reason for personal or communal efforts. When the functional becomes the ultimate purpose, people's deepest needs cannot be met and a superficial life results.

A full life balances ultimate and functional dynamics. To stress the ultimate and neglect the functional leads to aimlessness and irresponsibility; to emphasize the functional and neglect the ultimate leads to meaninglessness and loneliness. When either extreme occurs, alienation results.

Many facets of contemporary life fall under the functional. Work, money, technology, power, and problem solving often determine people's priorities and lifestyles. In such a world, play, prayer, religion, love, and community take a back seat.

Secular culture comes down heavily on the side of the functional. At times, this attitude also influences churches. When the latter occurs, church ministries often fail to touch people's deepest needs.

II. UNITED STATES CULTURE

Effective use of the *Catechism of the Catholic Church* requires a sensitive analysis of the ways ultimate and functional aspects of United States culture affect contemporary Catholics. The balance or imbalance of such ultimate and functional dimensions within today's culture can be analyzed in different ways. This chapter does so in light of certain characteristics of United States culture and people's current needs. Hopefully, this approach will help catechists, church ministers, and families better appreciate the underlying dynamics operative in the lives of those who are being catechized and to put into clearer focus how to use the insights of the *Catechism*.

Characteristics of Contemporary United States Culture

United States culture offers unique characteristics which flow from this country's history as a free people. Freedom has brought together a people from many different backgrounds, with race, ethnicity, class, and religion as significant components.

This culture is shifting dramatically as the United States expands into the global community, faces the immigrant influx, experiences increasing terror from crime, struggles with health care, witnesses growing poverty, and copes with the technological explosion.

United States culture is a complex blend of people's search for ultimate meaning within a functional lifestyle. It is not a neat package, but resembles a mosaic, and it includes seven key elements: diversity, freedom, individuality, mobility, materialism, technology, and moral insensitivity. Each suggests significant consequences for catechists who share Jesus' "Good News."

1. Diversity

Diversity is a hallmark of United States society. As a boy, when I shopped for a shirt, each store usually offered a selection of several styles. Today, I can choose between ten or twenty shirts in almost any store. If I wait a month, they will be replaced by more. It is enlightening to go a craft shop or flea market and see the thousands of trinkets to set around the home. Product selection is manifold whether this includes store-bought goods or television channels. On a human scale, diversity is apparent anytime people leave their homes. At a recent priest conference, various perspectives emerged from the fifteen different nationalities that were represented by the 150 priests in attendance.

Such diversity affects catechesis. On the one hand, many similar resources, like textbooks or visual aids, exist for catechists, each trying to gain a significant market share. Such availability can provide an easy excuse for catechists not to develop their own personal creativity. On the other hand, catechists face tremendous differences in the social and faith perspectives of those seeking to be catechized.

The diversity apparent throughout the United States invites catechists to cut through different approaches and root their catechesis in the Core Mode, centering it in Jesus Christ. In the words of the *Catechism,*

> The transmission of the Christian faith consists primarily in proclaiming Jesus Christ in order to lead others to faith in him. . . . In catechesis "Christ, the Incarnate Word and Son of God," . . . is taught—everything else is taught with reference to him.[66]

2. Freedom [67]

A superficial analysis of United States culture reveals a highly functional lifestyle, a deeper look reveals more. United States culture rests on the basic premise of human freedom, guaranteed by the Constitution. Few other countries give citizens and noncitizens the rights that this country gives them. These rights, sometimes drawn out endlessly in court systems, reflect belief in a person's inalienable right to life, liberty, and the pursuit of happiness.

Freedom is a cherished value. From colonial days, ethnic peoples arrived here hoping for freedom's dream. The ensuing mix formed a cultural pattern unique in world history. With this ethnic influx came distinctive lifestyles, challenges, and ways to approach issues. The Fourth of July celebrates such freedom, this country's most cherished treasure. A personal story illustrates this point. When I was a boy, my grandmother described the day she arrived in the New York harbor in a small sailing boat from Holland. As poor immigrants, her family spent the six-week voyage with the animals and supplies in the depths of the ship. She said, "As a small girl, tears streamed down my eyes when I saw the Statue of Liberty and I knew I was free."

---

[66] *Catechism of the Catholic Church,* #425, 427.

[67] This section uses the term "freedom" in a generic sense to include: (1) "core freedom," or an existential defining characteristic which follows one to actualize one's potential as a human being, and (2) "liberty," or the capacity in society to act out one's choices.

Freedom guarantees the right of individuals and churches to practice their religion of choice, something assumed in the United States. Free people react differently from those in totalitarian countries or even from those highly influenced by traditional ethnic values. This is evident in the ways different cultures deal with dissent. United States culture accepts different viewpoints as the right of free people. The freedom to disagree grounds this country's cultural reality; yet it does not threaten the basic fibre of culture. By contrast, nondemocratic institutions often see conflict, divergent views, and dissent as challenges to culture itself.

In the aftermath of Vatican II, cultural attitudes toward freedom in the United States affected Catholics. As the church moved to a more open society, many Catholics formed their own consciences on matters of morals, discipline, and belief. Some took seriously the teachings of the church; unfortunately, others did not.

As this happened, Catholics often scrutinized many theological, political, and social issues in light of their own personal attitudes and choices. This put great stress on church leaders, now faced with Catholics who often no longer agreed with their directives.

While celebrating the blessings of freedom, United States Catholics can use the *Catechism* to remind themselves,

> As long as freedom has not bound itself definitively to its ultimate good which is God, there is the possibility of *choosing between good and evil*, and thus of growing in perfection or of failing and sinning.
> There is no true freedom except in the service of what is good and just.[68]

These expressions imply that discipleship demands responsible freedom, which requires serious efforts to form a

---

[68] *Catechism of the Catholic Church*, #1732, 1733.

correct conscience by taking seriously church teaching. It also means knowing Jesus' teachings, and it requires the kind of trust in God that Jesus implies in Matthew's Gospel: "I tell you solemnly, unless you change and become like little children you will never enter the kingdom of heaven."[69]

Jesus demanded a childlike trust from his disciples. When such trust is given, the believer becomes free, for in sickness, or when faced with insuperable burdens or disappointments, the individual knows that God's support is there, as it was for Jesus on the cross. For the Christian, trust in God promises a freedom that the world cannot give.

Catechizing from the *Catechism of the Catholic Church* must take into account the freedom inherent in the mythos of United States Catholics. To be effective, teachings of the *Catechism* need to challenge Catholics to use their freedom in a responsible way. The *Catechism* can help Catholics to see that following the Lord does not mean accepting Catholic beliefs in an uncritical, childish way. Rather, it means prophetically looking at how the Lord leads them to salvation through the Catholic community and its teachings. This requires respecting the church's authority and each individual's conscience, while making sure that Catholics know what the church teaches and why.

Catechists are challenged to help people learn the positive teachings of the *Catechism of the Catholic Church*, link them with their freedom, and incorporate them into a supportive Catholic community.

3. Individuality[70]

Individuality goes hand-in-hand with freedom. It is a starting point that affirms the dignity of every person. In referring to this dignity, the *Catechism* says,

---

[69] Matthew 18:3.

[70] Individuality is not to be confused with individualism. The latter is self-centeredness, concern with oneself to the exclusion of others. Individuality, however, recognizes the importance of oneself but never minimizes other people.

Endowed with "a spiritual and immortal soul," the human person is "the only creature on earth that God willed for its own sake.". . . The human person participates in the light and power of the divine Spirit. [71]

United States Catholics cherish such individuality, which gives them insights into their personal uniqueness, for a free God creates a free people, made in the divine image. The church can help people discover their uniqueness before God and teach them how God gives different gifts to different people.

While the church encourages its members to acknowledge their individuality, it also needs to caution them about the negative effects of selfish individualism. The latter is a barrier to community and blocks Jesus' message of compassion, particularly for the less fortunate members of society.

The *Catechism*'s strong challenge to respect human rights and to develop loving Christian communities reminds Catholics of their obligation to respect individuality but oppose individualism, the latter being antithetical to the Christian message of love. As the *Catechism* says,

> The vocation of humanity is to show forth the image of God and to be transformed into the image of the Father's only Son. This vocation takes a personal form since each of us is called to enter into the divine beatitude; it also concerns the human community as a whole. . . . The human person needs to live in society. [72]

4. Mobility

From earliest times, Unites States citizens have been on the move. Impelled by a frontier spirit, they migrated from coastal regions to plains, mountains to deserts. This expansion continues into the new frontiers of space and ocean. Today, United

---

[71] *Catechism of the Catholic Church*, #1703, quoting *Gaudium et Spes*, and 1704.
[72] Ibid., #1877 and 1879.

States technology has opened up new frontiers, enabling persons of various cultures to communicate personally or electronically in ways not possible a generation ago.

It would be hard to live without the mobility made possible by automobiles, buses, and airplanes. Mobility has rearranged lifestyles and shifted support systems from extended families and neighbors to a country-wide network of families, colleagues, friends, and interest groups.

Contemporary people move often, thus requiring institutions to accommodate them. Such mobility presents a special challenge to parishes, for people who move often hesitate to get involved. The consequences for parish community and catechesis are profound. Since long-term contact is difficult for mobile people, it is important to encourage parishioners to find a stability in their faith that goes beyond the community of one particular parish. This type of stability is rooted in the Core Mode. Among the needs springing from this mode is the need for security and certitude.

One reason for the success of fundamentalist churches is their promise of such certitude, which they find in the Bible. Catholics need to take seriously fundamentalists' success and discover new ways to bring security and certitude to Catholics.[73]

Before Vatican II, Catholics found such certitude in the church. Today's Catholic certitude arises from three sources. There is (1) the certitude coming from the Scriptures, (2) the certitude flowing from Catholic teaching, and (3) the certitude springing from a reappreciation of community, authority, and church leaders.

The *Catechism* can encourage Catholics (1) to discover the certitude learned from the wisdom of the Scriptures, especially the teachings of Jesus; (2) to take seriously all church

---

[73] "Certitude" in this section is understood to mean "solid certitude," "moral certitude," and the "certitude of faith." Such certitude is not unthinking, blind acceptance, but one that is well-considered and reflective, based on confidence in Jesus and the church. It is not based on emotional fervor, for the Catholic Church has a two-thousand-year tradition of faith that seeks understanding.

teachings, but clarify essential teachings and distinguish them from those that are not central to the church's life and mission; and (3) to encourage church leaders to see that more is required to bring certitude to the Catholic community than the Scriptures and the *Catechism*. For certitude to return to the Catholic community, church leaders need to root their authority in the service dimensions of the Gospels, concentrate on the spiritual aspects of ministry, address realistically church problems, and assist the laity in taking their place in the church's life and ministry. Then the following words of the *Catechism* will ring true in the lives of mobile Catholics:

> Because the Holy Spirit is the anointing of Christ, it is Christ who, as the head of the Body, pours out the Spirit among his members to nourish, heal, and organize them in their mutual functions, to give them life, send them to bear witness, and associate them to his self-offering to the Father and to his intercession for the whole world.[74]

5. Materialism

In his parable about the man who planned to build bigger and bigger barns to hold his grain and material possessions, Jesus said,

> Fool! This very night, the demand will be made for your soul; and this hoard of yours, whose will it be then? [75]

These words challenge the materialistic lifestyle of many people in the United States. Such materialism holds up the latest automobile, clothes, or computer as necessary for a happy, successful life. Often, television advertising and programs imply that success and meaning are associated with pleasure, products, and possessions, implicitly suggesting that these can satisfy the deepest needs of the Core Mode. Materialism can blind

---

[74] *Catechism of the Catholic Church*, #739.
[75] Luke 12:20.

people to the needs of others in their own society and can make them poor global neighbors: by demanding many global resources for themselves, materialists deprive others in the world.

This materialistic philosophy often tempts people to concentrate on the functional rather than on the ultimate aspects of life. It is hard for religious educators to preach a message of altruism, sacrifice, and self-denial when people are deluged every day with a materialistic message.

In such a context, it is especially important for churches to counter this message through the images they project. In particular, this means concentrating on the spiritual and recalling the words of the *Catechism,*

> Jesus shares the life of the poor, from the cradle to the cross; he experiences hunger, thirst, and privation. Jesus identifies himself with the poor of every kind and makes active love toward them the condition for entering his kingdom.[76]

6. Technology

Technology has revolutionized the United States. Rapid transportation enables people to keep more accurate records, build safer buildings, develop comfortable work and living spaces, and communicate almost instantly through fax machines, interactive video, telephones, and computers. Advances in medicine and technology help people to live longer, travel worldwide in short time spans, communicate globally through television and computers, and enjoy the benefits of a free society. The United States sets the standard for fashions, music, and television programs. It is the leader of the global community of nations.

Such functional advances bless people in countless ways. For the first time in history, it is possible to overcome world hunger, if richer countries join poorer nations to share the abundance of food now harvestable because of modern fertilizers, seeds, and machinery.

---

[76] *Catechism of the Catholic Church,* #544.

These developments challenge Catholics to work for social justice, so that all peoples may benefit from the blessings of technology. In particular, catechists can help those being catechized realize that greater awareness of God and their own dignity helps them acknowledge their responsibilities to others. In this context, the *Catechism* says,

> An increased sense of God and increased self-awareness are fundamental to any *full development of human society*. This development multiplies material goods and puts them at the service of the person. . . . It reduces dire poverty and economic exploitation. It makes for growth in respect for cultural identities and openness to the transcendent.[77]

7. Moral Insensitivity

The diversity in United States culture often leads to conflicting positions on many matters. Contemporary society faces many quandaries resulting from such positions, which sometimes reflect opposing values and a lack of consistent moral glue to hold together society's fabric.

Hence, United States society often has difficulty finding a process to deal sufficiently with such conflicting and sometimes competing moral/ethical values. It cannot be counted on to reinforce the moral values of any one group.

For Catholics, now immersed in secular society, this affords positive and negative challenges; Catholics need well-cultivated skills in analytical reflection to sort out the values that bombard them.

Positive Challenges

The diversity of race, class, religion, and ethnicity brings untold blessings. Various cultures provide new energy and ways of acting while challenging old approaches. This dialogue of diversity invites the church to respect, welcome, and utilize the wisdom, knowledge, skills, and abilities of its various peoples and races.

---

[77] Ibid., #2441.

At the same time, United States culture challenges the faith community with serious issues which can provide the agenda for discussions among Catholics. These include:

- the issue of moral autonomy and community responsibility
- the relationship between church and state
- conflicts between the individual and common good
- integration of psychological insights about sexual development into considerations of sexual morality
- the role of the faith community in developing public policy on ethical issues

Addressing such issues is a positive way to allow culture to impact on morality and to develop moral themes in this historical time.

Negative Challenges

Diversity also brings with it the temptation to level ethical values. When this happens, many societal attitudes become inconsistent with the Judeo-Christian ethic. For example, some people seem to have lost their sense of sin and now restrict it to "getting caught." Until that happens, they do not impute responsibility to their actions and think little of cheating, stealing, defrauding a company, or having a sexual involvement with a work associate, neighbor, or acquaintance. For them, the sin is getting caught.

Many current television programs and commercials foster such a leveling of moral values, which is a widespread phenomenon in the United States, where corruption, injustice, or infidelity are not limited to television, and perversion does not stop with bizarre talk shows that look for the latest escapade to keep ratings high.

The attitude "I'm an adult and can do whatever I want" influences many Catholics. For example, young people often roll their eyes when a religion teacher tells them the church does not permit sexual activity outside of marriage. This contrasts with what they hear on TV, see on videotapes, and learn from friends.

Christians who resist negative secular influences may appear strangely irrelevant, but people often admire such irrelevance. Those who stand up for what they believe and live what they preach present a powerful witness to society. When, however, they succumb to negative materialistic values, they exercise little influence.

Countering moral insensitivity demands faithfulness to Jesus' and the church's moral teachings. While respecting the rights of individuals to form their consciences, catechists need to present clearly the church's teachings and help those being catechized learn how to form a correct conscience. In this regard, catechists do well to reflect on the words of the *Catechism*,

> But to do its work grace must uncover sin so as to convert our hearts and bestow on us "righteousness to eternal life through Jesus Christ our Lord." Like a physician who probes the wound before treating it, God, by his Word and by his Spirit, casts a living light on sin.[78]

III. CONTEMPORARY NEEDS

The characteristics described above set the stage for discussing the contemporary needs of United States people. These needs center around the meaning of life, intimacy, community, fulfillment beyond the functional, certitude, and credible authority.

The Search for Meaning in Life

Contemporary people search for meaning in their lives. This need, often unarticulated, is present in men, women, and children. What does life mean to a child whose family is torn apart by divorce, abuse, or drugs? To an adult whose work involves putting computerized parts into an impersonal system?

---

[78] Ibid., #1848.

To a college graduate who, after spending $60,000 to $100,00, for an education, cannot find work? To an eighty-year-old man in a nursing home, whose family never visits him?

People in such situations are blessed when they have faith and receive personal support from family and friends. But what about those without faith or personal support? It is no accident that today's suicide rate among young people is at an all-time high. Nor has the increase in gang membership happened by chance. These phenomena are symptomatic of a rootless generation bombarded with the message "This world's pleasures and money are all that count." They look for a way out of their loneliness.

The present situation offers the Catholic community an opportunity to respond to people's needs. In particular, it allows catechists to help those being catechized realize that ultimate meaning can be found only in God. For this to happen, catechists need to connect Jesus' teaching with the real situations of children, youth, and adults. In referring to creation and life's ultimate purpose, the *Catechism* reminds catechists that ultimate meaning can be found only by moving to the level of life's ultimate reality (Core Mode):

> "Where do we come from?" "Where are we going?" "What is our origin?" "What is our end?" "Where does everything that exists come from and where is it going?" The two questions, the first about the origin and the second about the end, are inseparable. They are decisive for the meaning and orientation of our life and actions.[79]

The Desire for Intimacy

Sally, a veteran second-grade teacher, described the differences between today's children and those of yesteryear. She said,

> The differences are profound. Today's kids are more sophisticated. They know a lot—often the wrong things,

---

[79] Ibid., #282.

learned from TV and personal experiences. They learn
about sex at an early age. Many come from dysfunctional
families. They are irritable, with short attentions spans.
I am struck by their desire for intimacy, coming from the
loneliness they feel at home. If I let them, many kids
would hang on me from the time they come to school
until they go home.

Youth and young adults reflect similar intimacy needs.
For them, sex, drinking, and drugs often are substitutes for intimacy. This is indicated in a young woman's remarks: "I really
don't enjoy sex that much, I'd rather just be friends. Often,
when I feel so lonely, drinking helps me forget this feeling."
Many older adults also turn to drink and illegitimate sexual
encounters when they fail to find satisfaction in their personal
lives and fast-paced, functional world.

Intimacy needs challenge churches to develop viable
youth ministry, small Christian communities, and support
groups. A catechist cannot teach effectively if the intimacy
needs of those being catechized are overlooked, as if the teacher
were filling up an empty container.

The Quest for Community

"Community" is used here in a broad sense to include family
and other human associations that have the ultimate as an
important component of the relationships between their members.[80] In this sense, family is the paradigm of all communities.
The *Catechism* describes the family as a "privileged community
called to achieve a 'sharing of thought and common deliberation
by the spouses as well as their eager cooperation as parents in
the children's upbringing.'"[81] In a loving family, everyday life

[80] Community happens when two or more persons relate regularly and responsibly
on an ultimate level. The dynamics that keep community together tend toward
the ultimate, whereas groups or organizations tend toward the functional.
Communities, unlike groups or organizations, cannot be created artificially,
for the former develop out of the relationships of their members.
[81] *Catechism of the Catholic Church*, #2206, quoting *Gaudium et Spes*.

fosters ongoing relationships that solidify human bonding and enable persons to relate in a responsible way. In healthy families the members know they will be supported in successes and failures.

Changing family patterns present challenges today. Working parents, out-of-town business trips, children's activities, shopping after work, eating at fast-food restaurants, single parent and blended families indicate why many family members find it difficult to experience adequate quantity and quality time with one another.

Not finding their needs met at home, people often look elsewhere for community. Many find legitimate ways to fulfill this need—small church gatherings, youth groups, and suchlike. Others find their outlets in drugs, unhealthy group associations, questionable friends, or illicit affairs.

Parishes, Catholic schools, and other church gatherings can reach out to people who have this need for community. In particular, catechetical sessions and liturgical functions afford church ministers the opportunity to draw people into the parish community.

In addition to providing opportunities for community within the confines of various church gatherings, parishes serve their members by affirming nonparish environments where people find community. Such environments include neighborhood or family gatherings, work situations, study or support groups, sports activities, assemblies, civic meetings, and retirement homes. Often, God is found in such places, and the church helps its members by reminding them of these opportunities to experience God's presence and serve their brothers and sisters.

The Need for Fulfillment Beyond the Functional

People, unfulfilled by functional living, search for the ultimate in their quest for love, peace, quiet time, or quiet space. But when they look for the ultimate in a church setting and discover functional organizations, efficient programs, and money concerns, but little in the way of spiritual nourishment, they often become disillusioned. In fact, contacting a pastoral minister sometimes requires considerable effort getting through secretaries, housekeepers, and answering machines.

The current need for fulfillment beyond the functional invites parish ministers, including catechists, to reexamine the way that Jesus treated people. He took time with them, was sensitive to their needs, and taught them their personal worth before God. People seek the same response from our parishes, a response that must be inspired by the Holy Spirit. As the *Catechism* says,

> The Holy Spirit is the protagonist, "the principal agent of the whole of the Church's mission." It is he who leads the Church on her missionary paths. "This mission continues and, in the course of history, unfolds the mission of Christ, who was sent to evangelize the poor; so the Church, urged on by the Spirit of Christ, must walk the road Christ himself walked, a way of poverty and obedience, of service and self-sacrifice even to death, a death from which he emerged victorious by his resurrection."[82]

For catechesis, this means centering catechetical instruction, activities, and service around the Paschal Mystery. From the dying and rising of Jesus all parish ministry receives its dynamism and hope.

The Yearning for Certitude and Roots

Uncertainties about job, family, employment, and living situation, which cross all ages and socio-economic strata, indicate the need for certitude and roots. During uncertain times, certitude and roots help people ground their search for intimacy, meaning, and fulfillment beyond the functional.

The question "How can the Catholic Church provide certitude and roots for her members?" rarely has been asked. How the Catholic Church addresses this question will affect its

---

[82] Ibid., #852, quoting from John Paul II, *R Miss 21* and *Ad Gentes 5*.

vitality in the new millennium. All serious efforts to deal with
this question must center around the Core and Community
Modes. Approaching it from the Consideration Mode is not the
best way to begin.

The *Catechism of the Catholic Church* fits into the
Consideration Mode. It can contribute some answers to the
above mentioned question, but these contributions can bring
certitude only when genuine conviction and common purpose
already exist in the larger Catholic community and when the
teachings of the *Catechism* ring true in the common experience
of Catholic people.

The Desire for Credible Authority

Lack of respect for civic and church authorities is a modern
tragedy. Gone is the mystique, awe, and admiration surrounding
them. Many in authority have betrayed the public's trust
through scandals, questionable politics, and the inability to cope
with real issues.

Authority and leadership are not the same. A person in
office, like a judge or pastor, has authority by virtue of his or her
appointment. A person becomes a leader when he or she is recognized by a group as its leader. A pastor or a president of a country
may have authority but may never be an effective leader.

In the pre-Vatican II church, where leadership was associated with authority, people usually respected the opinions and
followed the directives of church authorities. Today, the same is
not always true.

The ramifications of this changing attitude toward
church authority are profound for catechesis. Many people
question the church's political, social, and moral stances and disagree on issues such as the age for first reconciliation or
confirmation, the ordination of married men, and medical-moral
issues. Recent scandals involving bishops and priests have eroded
public confidence in church authority, especially when people
sensed a cover-up, or a lack of honesty or failure to support

victims. This climate makes it difficult for church leaders to lead and for catechists to uphold the church's teachings on morality, fidelity in marriage, and a host of other issues.

Coupled with problems facing the church because of these recent scandals is the challenge presented by the declining number of priests. The real fibre of church leadership in the contemporary church will be measured by how well church authorities face this issue, which is beginning to tear asunder the heart of United States Catholicism. Without priests, how will the dying be anointed? Who will minister the sacrament of reconciliation? This is in addition to the weakening or cessation of Sunday liturgies in many places. And the question is not just, "How many priests are needed?, but even more important, "What is the quality of the priests?"

The above issues are primarily church, not catechetical, problems. This point becomes crucial when addressing the best way to teach the basic messages contained in the *Catechism*.

This chapter has considered key cultural dynamics, characteristics of United States culture, and significant needs of people today. The ability of the church to relate to the present situation in which it finds itself will affect significantly the catechetical success of the *Catechism*.

CHAPTER FOUR

FUTURE SUGGESTIONS IN LIGHT OF THE *CATECHISM OF THE CATHOLIC CHURCH*

I n his "Introduction" to the *Catechism of the Catholic Church*, Pope John Paul II says,

> I declare [the *Catechism of the Catholic Church*] to be a sure norm for teaching the faith and thus a valid and legitimate instrument for ecclesial communion. May it serve the renewal to which the Holy Spirit ceaselessly calls the Church of God, the Body of Christ, on her pilgrimage to the undiminished light of the Kingdom![83]

For the *Catechism* to produce abundant fruit in the renewal of United States Catholicism, catechists will have to take into account two major factors, described in the previous chapters, that affected catechesis after Vatican II. The **first** was the movement to an open society. This brought with it new ways of bringing the Christian message into relationship with individuals and parishes. The 1970s and 1980s introduced various methods to accomplish this purpose. The 1990s afford the church a chance to refine the most effective ways to catechize in light of the *Catechism of the Catholic Church*. The **second** was the recognition of the significance of cultural influences in the lives of Catholics and the importance of relating catechesis to the cultures involved.

---

[83] *Catechism of the Catholic Church*, #3.

These two factors imply consequences for catechesis. This chapter, which offers suggestions in light of the *Catechism of the Catholic Church*, is divided into four sections: (1) The *Catechism* and Broader Church Issues, (2) The *Catechism*, Culture, and People's Situations; (3) The *Catechism*, Content, and Method; and (4) Using the *Catechism*.

I. *CATECHISM OF THE CATHOLIC CHURCH* AND BROADER CHURCH ISSUES

The *Catechism of the Catholic Church* affords Catholics an opportunity to reexamine the meaning of being a Catholic. As previously mentioned, the Catholic identity question involves church and culture issues and cannot be solved by catechesis or the use of the *Catechism* alone.

Catholic Identity

Teaching Catholics the basics of their faith will not solve the Catholic identity question nor usher in a return to the loyalty that an older generation experienced before Vatican II. More is required. Addressing pressing concerns like the impact of secular values on families, justice issues, liturgical renewal, people's spiritual hunger, women's issues in the church, and the shortage of celibate priests will be necessary if the church hopes to reestablish a solid groundwork for ascertaining what it means to be a Catholic in the twenty-first century.

The *Catechism* can occasion a deeper consideration of such matters if it moves the larger church community, especially church leaders, to focus on the deepest spiritual, catechetical, liturgical, and service dimensions of the Gospel as these relate to people at home, at work, at play, in their neighborhoods, and in their churches.

While many Catholics make heroic efforts to share their faith, parishes need to reach out to parishioners who are Catholic in name only. More and more families do not attend church, pray together, or put faith symbols, like the crucifix or a picture of Mary, in their homes. The number of children from such families, who now enter Catholic school and out-of-school religion programs, grows. The *Catechism* provides an opportunity to refocus on the home as basic to a person's faith formation and to do more to teach young people and adults the basic truths of the faith in ways that make sense to them.

While the *Catechism* offers many opportunities to revitalize catechesis, it will not cure every ill, for inadequate religious education cannot be blamed for all the church's problems. The *Catechism* is not going to improve catechesis in isolation, for a catechist's effectiveness is influenced by the overall spirit of the parish and the family situations of those being catechized.

Hence a catechist alone cannot influence significantly a parish's hospitality or the situation of children who come for catechesis. In other words, catechists do not have total control over catechesis, and they have to learn to live with this fact.

Synthesis of Catholic Belief

In addition to challenging Catholics to reconsider the identity question, the *Catechism* affords the church community an opportunity to look more seriously at ways to teach basic Catholic beliefs. To accomplish this purpose, the *Catechism* is divided into four main books: "The Profession of Faith," "The Sacramental Celebration of the Paschal Mystery," "Life in Christ," and "Christian Prayer." Stressing the basic church teaching in these books will help overcome the fuzziness that surrounded religion teaching after Vatican II.

Yet despite its role in clarifying basic Catholic teaching, the *Catechism* is not to be seen as a "club" to insist that a particular belief must be taught in "this way" alone. Many catechists fear that if this happens, they will be on the firing line from those who will insist on checking their teaching in light of the *Catechism*. Such an inquisition-like approach will fracture the Catholic community and do no good to improve the quality of catechesis.

On the other hand, the *Catechism* can be a valuable reference work in coordinating catechetical content as textbook publishers develop books, catechetical leaders devise a consistent and complete plan for a doctrinally balanced catechetical program, and catechists prepare to teach their classes.

II. *CATECHISM OF THE CATHOLIC CHURCH*, CULTURE, AND PEOPLE'S SITUATIONS

People never respond to catechesis in a vacuum, for their core and community experiences are the lenses through which they interpret what they look for and what they hear. Consequently, catechists are invited to devise ways to relate the *Catechism of the Catholic Church* to the needs of contemporary Catholics of any age, culture, or circumstance.

United States Culture

The unique characteristics of United States culture, especially diversity, individuality, and mobility, present special challenges to catechists. From earliest years, people need to understand that Jesus' teaching gives them a blueprint for life. Sometimes, this means challenging their values or the values around them. At other times, it means working as a partner with God to help build a more just world.

Catechists provide a valuable service when they relate the catechetical message to the situations of those being catechized. This might mean encouraging children to put out an elderly neighbor's garbage each week without pay. For adolescents, it might mean refusing to go along with the social pressure of premarital sex. For adults, it might mean taking a job that pays less money in order to be home more with one's family.

Personal Dimension

Catechists need to deal with the questions that children, youth, and adults ask, not to answer questions they have not yet asked. This does not imply that catechists should avoid teachings that deal with future, rather than immediate, concerns. It does mean, however, that catechists are to teach in an understandable and meaningful way the aspects of faith that will have future significance to those being catechized.

There must be a personal dimension in every catechetical session, even if this is no more than acknowledging a person's present state. This is important when dealing with particular situations: children whose parents are seriously ill, or parents who grieve over the drug addiction of a child. When catechists show compassion and understanding, people are more able to understand God's movements in their lives. Taking a lesson from Jesus, there was a time when he consoled and a time when he formally taught. The catechist is called to do the same.

III. THE *CATECHISM OF THE CATHOLIC CHURCH,* CONTENT, AND METHODS

The *Catechism* continues in the tradition of church teachings that are rooted in Jesus' story. For it to be effective, the *Catechism* needs to take its dynamism from his message. Viewing the *Catechism* within the context of Jesus' story has profound consequences for the way it is used to teach the basics of the faith.

Jesus' Story

The content of the *Catechism* needs to center on "Jesus' story" as revealed in the Christian Scriptures. Consequently, top priority must be given to teaching this story. The *Catechism* is not the Catholic Bible; the Hebrew and Christian Scriptures are. The *Catechism* must complement catechetical efforts to teach the Scriptures. It can be a valuable way to enhance them and show how the Catholic community interprets them.

The Scriptures are an integral part of catechesis. They help illuminate a person's situation as he or she reflects upon personal experiences and gets new insights from the Christian story. The catechist needs to do more, however, than teach the Scriptures. The Christian Scriptures came from the beliefs of the early church. These beliefs, clarified and refined over the centuries, set a clear direction for life. The catechist is invited to present the basic teachings of the larger Catholic story in an understandable way.

For this to happen, the catechist needs to be a person of prayer and faith, able to decipher what are the basic teachings contained in the Catholic story. In reference to the *Catechism*, all of its teachings are true, but some truths are more basic than others. The catechist's yardstick to discern the most basic truths must be magisterial teaching and how closely various teachings relate to the central biblical teachings in Jesus' story, for example: teachings about the reign of God, Jesus, salvation, poverty, morality, prayer, social justice, Jesus' redemptive death, his resurrection, eternal life, church, sacraments, and Mary. The catechist who identifies the basic teachings of Jesus' story, as this story is interpreted faithfully by the Catholic Church, will identify the basic teachings of the *Catechism*.

Just as Jesus' story is best seen as an organic whole in light of the resurrection, so does the *Catechism* need to be seen in its entirety as a valuable contribution summarizing basic Catholic belief. The *Catechism* says,

> This catechism is conceived as an organic presentation of the Catholic faith in its entirety. It should be seen therefore as a unified whole. Numerous cross-references in the margin of the text (italicized numbers referring to other paragraphs that deal with the same theme), as well as the analytical index at the end of the volume, allow the reader to view each theme in its relationship with the entirety of the faith.[84]

This is the spirit in which the *Catechism of the Catholic Church* was written. To insure its organic unity, the *Catechism*

---

[84] Ibid., #18.

cross-references the various parts of the text. One does it a disservice when taking phrases out of context to prove a point.

Hence, the *Catechism* is a valuable resource which can help catechists, teachers, pastors, bishops, textbook publishers, and students clarify the basic teachings in the Jesus story and the teachings of the Catholic Church.

Content and Method

The *Catechism* challenges catechists, catechetical leaders, and textbook publishers to blend solid catechetical methods with the basic teachings contained in the *Catechism*. This means learning a lesson from the past that whenever content or method are overemphasized, inadequate catechesis results.

The pre-Vatican II church placed a strong emphasis on content. The catechism memorization method was effective as long as the church remained a relatively closed society. Its limitations showed up when the church moved to a more open stance. A strong emphasis on more experiential methods followed after Vatican II. Sometimes, these methods produced Catholics who learned about God's love, Jesus' friendship, and the church as community, but who were unclear about other key elements in the Catholic tradition.

The *Catechism* challenges Catholic publishers and catechists to balance content and method, seeing them as a both/and, not an either/or. Without such balance of content and method, catechesis will remain weak and incomplete, failing to meet the needs of today's Catholics.

The best guarantee to insure balanced catechesis comes from committed Catholic families, well-prepared catechists, and good pastoral oversight. Since catechesis begins in families and requires family support, parishes need to stress family-focused religious education and encourage parental support when children go to Catholic schools or parish schools of religion.

Successful, balanced catechetical programs usually come from good catechetical leadership of a parish coordinator/director of religious education. This person is entrusted with coordinating a staff of prepared, faithful catechists who know the basics of the Catholic faith and how to teach them. Such a catechetical leader supports, assists, and encourages catechists, while providing solid catechetical materials and offering ample opportunities for catechists in service programs.

Finally, pastoral oversight is required to insure that a catechetical program is solid and integrated within the broader parish ministerial context. The pastor, in particular, is responsible for this task. After Vatican II, the pastor often turned catechesis over to someone else and maintained only a passing contact with it. The time has come for pastors to get more directly involved in catechesis, which is a major part of the pastor's responsibility. Where the pastor works closely with catechists and catechetical leaders, good opportunities exist for a balanced religious education program.

IV. USING THE *CATECHISM OF THE CATHOLIC CHURCH*

When using the *Catechism* to further the conversion process, people need to remember that this process includes three dimensions, namely, the Core, Community, and Consideration Modes. To help those being catechized in their journey of faith, the catechist needs to take each of these modes into account.

Facilitator of Reflection

The catechist often serves as a facilitator of reflection in attempting to help those being catechized to appreciate Jesus' message and the church's teachings in their lives. For this reflection to respond most fully to people's needs, the catechist must be cognizant of all three modes involved in the conversion process and appreciate the importance of prayer in every catechetical endeavor.

The catechist has little control over the Core Mode, which is rooted in the relationship between the person and God. At the same time, the catechist can create a positive personal and group environment, not unlike the milieu that Jesus created, where people can experience God's mercy, love, and forgiveness.

The catechist can influence the Community Mode. This mode pertains primarily to the family, parish, or personal environment. Once again, however, the catechist can create a prayerful catechetical setting which becomes a Christian community in miniature. The environment that a catechist creates is crucial to what those being catechized hear as they listen and respond to God's Word.

Presuming efforts are made to reach the ultimate level in the first two modes, the catechist ministers most effectively within the third or Consideration Mode, when he or she instructs those being catechized in the basic teachings of the Catholic faith. This happens when the catechist teaches the Catholic basics in such a way as to move people to deepen their knowledge and love of God. For this reason, a catechist's knowledge and skills need to be honed, so that the *Catechism* can contribute to this reflection process.

Basic Symbols

In using the *Catechism*, pastors, catechetical leaders, and catechists need to remember that faith involves the whole person, not just an accumulation of knowledge. Faith is a free gift of God, which knowledge, in itself, cannot elicit.

God chooses to offer faith through the world of nature and people. Basic to this revelation is the symbolic way that people communicate through words, gestures, art, and environments that create a sense of the holy.

It's easy in the rational world of computers and technology to forget the human need for symbols. This has particular implications for the *Catechism*. In reassessing the future of catechesis in light of it, it is important to find ways to reemphasize basic faith symbols which signify Jesus' crucifixion, resurrection, and continued presence in the Christian community.

For centuries, the strength of Catholicism rested in its symbol system and its celebration of faith in art, architecture, liturgy, and life. As the church approaches the twenty-first century, time has come to refocus on basic faith symbols, including the saints—those holy men and women who continually inspire Catholics to follow Jesus. Parents and religious educators are encouraged to use Catholic symbols to deepen the faith of those being catechized.

Specific Suggestions in Using the *Catechism of the Catholic Church*

To enhance the use of the *Catechism*, the following suggestions are recommended:

1. The *Catechism*'s emphasis on prayer in catechesis is a strong reminder to catechists that prayer is an integral part of all catechetical activities.

2. Basic teachings of the *Catechism* need to be incorporated within the personal and individual situations of those being catechized. When this happens in various ethnic cultures and among different age and socio-economic groups, Catholics can see that basic church teachings remain the same, even though they are manifested differently in different cultures.

3. The *Catechism* offers adult learners an opportunity to devise varying ways to use the *Catechism* in facilitating ongoing conversion.

4. The *Catechism* challenges catechists to engage in lifelong learning which will facilitate their continuing conversion.

5. The publication of the *Catechism* provides an opportunity for parish directors of religious education to remember that they are integral links between pastors, parents, and adults.

6. The *Catechism* invites bishops and pastors to take steps to insure that effective catechesis happens in their dioceses and parishes. During the 1970s and 1980s, bishops often turned

over many catechetical responsibilities to others. Today, the *Catechism* provides them a new opportunity to oversee and support catechetical activities.

7. The *Catechism* is a key resource to be used in courses for catechist certification.

8. Diocesan catechetical offices are encouraged to develop or revise their graded courses of study and curriculum guidelines in light of the *Catechism*.

9. Those using the *Catechism* need to remember that the "In Brief" summaries at the end of each section do not contain necessarily the most important points in the section. Some summaries contain the main items treated in the sections. Others, however, contain new points not previously treated in the section.

10. Publishers are encouraged to indicate the correlation between the *Catechism* and textbook materials, taking culture, effective methodology, and faith development into consideration.

11. Anyone using the *Catechism* is challenged to use the Jesus story as the groundwork for maintaining a balance between content and method in teaching the "Good News" of God's love.

12. Individual passages or statements in the *Catechism* need to be interpreted within their proper context, in light of the teachings of Vatican II, and according to solid Catholic biblical and theological scholarships.

After Pentecost, Jesus' disciples compiled the central dynamic of his teachings into the Beatitudes, which reflect the heart of Christian discipleship. They are a constant reminder of the basic message of Jesus' teachings. In using the *Catechism of the Catholic Church*, Catholics are invited to return to the Beatitudes to insure that their teachings reflect the spirit of Jesus.

As the church moves into the twenty-first century, the *Catechism of the Catholic Church* affords Catholics an opportunity to reexamine the meaning of being Catholic and to look at what must be done to teach people the basic truths of the faith in ways that make sense to them. The ability of the church to be true to Jesus' teachings, while addressing catechetical challenges, will influence its effectiveness in moving people to accept Christ.

In this endeavor, Jesus remains the model for all catechetical efforts. He proclaimed "Good News" and entrusted the continuation of this ministry to his church. This requires humility, forgiveness, and patience, couched in a firm conviction that no catechetical renewal can happen in the Catholic Church unless the church centers her ministry around Jesus' message of the reign of God. This message touches every person's spiritual core, where the individual meets God in prayer.

Therefore, let the church's renewal of catechetical ministry focus on prayer, as Catholics remember the words of the *Catechism.*

The drama of prayer is fully revealed to us in the Word who
became flesh and dwells among us . . . . The Son of God who
became Son of the Virgin learned to pray in his human heart.
He learned it from his mother, who kept all the great things
the Almighty had done for her and treasured them in her
heart.[85]

The Catholic Church puts her catechetical renewal
under the guidance of Mary, as indicated in Pope John Paul II's
introduction to the *Catechism of the Catholic Church*:

At the conclusion of this document presenting the *Catechism
of the Catholic Church*, I beseech the Blessed Virgin Mary,
Mother of the Incarnate Word and Mother of the Church, to
support with her powerful intercession the catechetical work
of the entire Church on every level, at this time when she is
called to a new effort of evangelization.[86]

---

[85] Ibid., #2598, 2599.

[86] Ibid., Introduction, #3.